PUMPKIN LOVERS COOK BOOK

More than 175 recipes for cookies, cakes, pies, muffins, breads, soups and other delights. Pumpkin facts and carving tips, too!

GOLDEN WEST ☼ PUBLISHERS

Cover photo by Dick Dietrich

Edited by Betty B. Gabbert

Printed in the United States of America

ISBN #0-914846-68-X

17th printing © 2006

Golden West Publishers
4113 N. Longview Ave.
Phoenix, AZ 85014, USA
(800) 658-5830

For free sample recipes and complete Table of Contents for every Golden West cookbook, visit: **www.goldenwestpublishers.com**

Favorite Pumpkin Recipes

Introduction

FAVORITE PUMPKIN RECIPES is a blend of old and new. Contained herein are recipes in their original form, just as they were submitted to our editors. This is the spirit that we wanted to preserve. Cooking with pumpkins should be a creative endeavor. Let your own creativeness show through. Each recipe variation has its own charm and flavor. Use these recipes as guidelines. Try several different pumpkin pie recipes and see which you and your family like best.

Pumpkins aren't just for Halloween and Thanksgiving. Better farming and harvesting techniques make whole pumpkins more readily available and pumpkins can be enjoyed year-round through the use of canned pumpkin products.

Today pumpkins are used in many different ways. Pumpkins are featured in recipes for salads, main dishes, desserts, breads, cakes, pies and candies. The seeds can be roasted and eaten. The pumpkin shells have long been a standard at Halloween, when children and adults delight in creating Jack-o'-Lanterns.

Pumpkins represent a unique facet of Americana. Indians were using pumpkins long before Columbus came to America, and certainly the pilgrims were delighted to discover the many pumpkin possibilities.

Included throughout this book are interesting snippets of information about pumpkins; the history, the use, the propagation. Also included are tips for carving pumpkins, and we've listed information on Pumpkin Festivals around America.

Let us know which recipes are your favorites. Let us know if you have pumpkin recipes we should include in the next edition. If you send us a recipe we use, we'll send you a free copy of the next edition of FAVORITE PUMPKIN RECIPES.

Breads, Rolls and Muffins

Easy Pumpkin Bread

2 cups buttermilk
   pancake mix
3/4 cup firmly packed
   brown sugar
1/2 tsp. nutmeg
1/2 tsp. cloves
1/4 tsp. ginger

1 cup cooked pumpkin
1/3 cup vegetable oil
1/4 cup milk
2 eggs, slightly beaten
1 tsp. cinnamon
1/2 cup chopped walnuts

Combine first 10 ingredients in a large mixing bowl. Beat 3 minutes at medium speed of an electric mixer. Stir in walnuts. Spoon batter into a greased 9 x 5 x 3 inch loaf pan. Bake 350° for 45 to 55 minutes or till a wooden pick inserted in center comes out clean. Cool in pan for 10 minutes. Remove from pan and cool completely.

World Pumpkin Weigh-Off winners are approaching the 1000 pound pumpkin!

Basic Pumpkin Bread

2 cups canned pumpkin
2 1/2 cups sugar
1 cup vegetable oil
1/3 cup water
4 eggs
1 cup chopped nuts

3 1/2 cups flour
1 tsp. cinnamon
1 tsp. nutmeg
1 1/2 tsp. salt
6 tsp. baking powder

Combine all ingredients in large mixing bowl and blend well. Divide dough into 3 well greased and floured 1 pound coffee cans. Bake 1 hour at 350°. Cool 10 minutes and remove from cans. Makes 3 loaves.

Pumpkin-Oatmeal Loaf

1 cup quick-cooking
  oats, uncooked
1 cup finely chopped
  dates
1 cup chopped raisins
1 cup chopped pecans
1 1/2 cups hot milk
2 eggs, beaten
1 tsp. vanilla

1/2 cup canned pumpkin
2 cups flour
3/4 cup sugar
1 Tbsp. plus 1 tsp.
  baking powder
1 tsp. salt
1 tsp. cinnamon
1/4 tsp. nutmeg

Combine oats, dates, raisins, pecans and milk; mix well and let stand 10 minutes. Stir in vanilla, eggs and pumpkin. Combine remaining ingredients; mix well and gradually stir into oat mixture. Spoon into greased and floured 9 x 5 x 3 inch loaf pan. Bake at 350° for 1 hour and 5 minutes or till wooden pick inserted in center comes out clean. Cool on wire rack.

Tip: to prevent fruit and nuts from sinking to bottom of bread or cake batter, shake them in a bag with a small amount of flour to dust lightly before adding to batter.

Pumpkin Skillet Cornbread

2 cups cornmeal
1 cup cooked pumpkin
1 tsp. baking soda
1/2 tsp salt
1 Tbsp. sugar

1 cup buttermilk
1 cup water
3 Tbsp. shortening or oil
1 egg, beaten

Mix cornmeal and pumpkin. Add baking soda, salt and sugar to buttermilk. Add water and add to cornmeal-pumpkin mixture. Add shortening and egg and mix well. Pour into greased iron skillet and bake in 400° oven for 35-45 minutes or until lightly browned. Serve hot with butter.

Pumpkin Pone

2 cups pumpkin
grated rind of 1 lemon
small bit of orange peel,
  grated very fine
4 eggs
1 teacupful butter

1 teacupful brown sugar
1 teacupful molasses
1/2 tsp. nutmeg
1/2 tsp. cloves
1/2 tsp. cinnamon
1 teacupful milk

Mix pumpkin, rind of lemon and orange. Beat eggs well, beat butter, sugar and molasses till creamy; add eggs, beat well and add pumpkin, spices and milk, beat all well together. Put mixture in a well buttered pan and bake slowly for about 1 hour. May be served hot or cold. Cut in slices.

Pumpkins mature in about 120 days.

Raised Pumpkin Bread

3 1/4 to 3 1/2 cups flour
2 pkgs. active dry yeast
1/2 tsp. ginger
1/4 tsp. nutmeg
1/4 tsp. cloves
3/4 cup milk

1/4 cup packed brown
  sugar
2 Tbsp. butter
1 1/2 tsp. salt
1/2 cup canned pumpkin
3/4 cup raisins

In large bowl, thoroughly combine 1 1/2 cups flour, yeast and spices. In pan, heat milk, sugar, butter and salt just till warm (115°-120°) stirring constantly to melt butter. Add to dry mixture. Add pumpkin. Beat at low speed with electric mixer for 1/2 minute scraping sides of bowl constantly. Beat 3 minutes at high speed. By hand, stir in raisins and enough of the remaining flour to make a moderately stiff dough. Turn onto lightly floured surface and knead till smooth and elastic (5-8 minutes). Shape into ball. Place in lightly greased bowl, turning once; cover and let rise in warm place till double (about 1 hour). Punch down; cover and let rest 10 minutes. Shape into loaf; place in greased 8 1/2 x 4 1/2 x 2 1/2 inch loaf pan. Cover; let rise till double (about 30 minutes). Bake at 375° for 35 to 40 minutes. Remove from pan.

Pumpkin Coconut Bread

2 cups flour
1 1/2 cups sugar
1 tsp. cinnamon
1 tsp. soda
2 cups pumpkin

4 well-beaten eggs
1/4 cup oil
2 pkgs (3 oz. ea.) Jell-O®
  coconut cream pie
  filling

Mix all ingredients together. Pour into 2 loaf pans. Bake at 375° for 1 hour.

Raised Pumpkin Seed-Wheat Bread

4 3/4 to 5 1/4 cups
   whole wheat flour
2 pkgs. active dry yeast
2 1/3 cups milk
1/2 cup honey

2 Tbsp. oil
1 Tbsp. salt
1 cup pumpkin seeds,
   coarsely chopped

In large bowl, combine 2 cups flour and the yeast. In pan, heat milk, honey, oil and salt just till warm (115°-120°). Add to dry mixture. Beat at low speed with electric mixer for 1/2 minute scraping sides of bowl constantly. Beat 3 minutes at high speed. By hand, stir in pumpkin seed and enough of the remaining flour to make a soft dough. Turn onto lightly floured board and knead till smooth and elastic (about 10 minutes). Shape into a ball. Place in lightly greased bowl, turning once to grease surface. Cover. Let rise in warm place till double (about 2 hours). Punch dough down, turn on lightly floured surface. Divide in half. Cover, let rest 10 minutes. Shape into 2 loaves and place in 2 greased 8 1/2 x 4 1/2 x 2 1/2 inch loaf pans. Cover and let rise till double (about 1 1/2 hour). Bake at 375° about 45 minutes. If browns too quickly, cover loosely with foil last 15 minutes. Remove bread from pans and cool on wire rack.

Whole Wheat Pumpkin Bread

2 1/2 cups honey
1 cup oil
2 eggs
1 large can pumpkin
2 1/2 cups sifted
   unbleached flour
2 1/2 cups sifted whole
   wheat flour

4 tsp. cloves
1 tsp. cinnamon
1/2 tsp. salt
6 tsp. baking powder
1 cup water
2 cups chopped nuts
2 cups raisins, optional

Mix together first 4 ingredients. Add dry ingredients alternating with water. Add nuts and raisins. Bake 1 hour at 350° in 3 loaf pans.

Fruit 'N Nut Pumpkin Bread

3 cups flour
1/2 tsp. baking powder
1 tsp. baking soda
1 tsp. ground nutmeg
1 tsp. ground cloves
1 tsp. ground cinnamon
1/2 tsp. salt

3 cups sugar
1 cup vegetable oil
3 eggs
1 (16 oz.) can pumpkin
1 cup raisins
1 cup nuts

Preheat oven to 350°. Grease a 10 inch fluted tube pan or two 8 x 4 inch loaf pans with unsalted shortening and dust with flour. Sift flour, baking powder, baking soda, nutmeg, cloves, cinnamon and salt. In another bowl, put sugar, oil and eggs and stir until blended. Stir pumpkin into egg mixture. Gradually add sifted dry ingredients to egg mixture, stirring well after each addition. Fold raisins and nuts into batter. Pour batter in pans. Bake 1 1/4 hours. (For loaf pans, decrease by 15 minutes.) Cool on rack 10 minutes. Remove from pans. Freezes well.

Buttermilk Pumpkin Bread

2 sticks margarine
2 3/4 cup sugar
3 eggs
2 cups pumpkin
1 tsp. cinnamon
1/2 tsp. nutmeg
1 tsp. allspice

3 1/2 cups flour
1 tsp. baking powder
1 tsp. soda
1 tsp. salt
2 tsp. vanilla
1/2 cup buttermilk

Blend margarine and sugar, add eggs (well beaten). Add pumpkin. Sift dry ingredients, add alternately with milk and vanilla. Add nuts if desired. Bake in greased and floured loaf pans at 350° about 1 hour.

Cranberry Pumpkin Bread

2 slightly beaten eggs
2 cups sugar
1/2 cup oil
1 cup pumpkin
2 1/4 cups flour

1 Tbsp. pumpkin pie
  spice
1 tsp. baking soda
1/2 tsp. salt
1 cup chopped cranberries

Combine first 4 ingredients; mix well. Combine flour, spice, baking soda and salt in large bowl. Add pumpkin mixture, stir until dry ingredients are moistened. Stir in cranberries. Spoon batter into 2 greased and floured 8 x 3 3/4 x 2 1/2 inch aluminum loaf pans. Bake at 350° for 1 hour or till toothpick inserted in center comes out clean. Makes 2 loaves.

> *The pumpkin plant is tropical in origin and grows only in warm weather. Two or three seeds should be planted two inches deep in hills six feet apart, or interplant with corn.*

Hickory Nut Pumpkin Bread

1 3/4 cups flour
1 tsp. baking soda
3/4 tsp. salt
1/2 tsp. cinnamon
1/2 tsp. nutmeg
1 1/2 cups sugar

1/2 cup shortening
3/4 cup cooked pumpkin
2 eggs
1/3 cup cold water
1 cup hickory nuts

Sift flour, baking soda, salt, cinnamon and nutmeg and set aside. Cream sugar and shortening and stir in pumpkin. Beat eggs and stir in cold water. Fold in dry ingredients and mix well, then add nuts. Pour into a 5 x 9 inch loaf pan and bake at 350° for about 1 hour. Can dribble a butter-sugar icing over top and sides.

Pumpkin Walnut Bread

1 cup packed brown
   sugar
1/3 cup shortening
2 eggs
1 cup canned pumpkin
1/4 cup milk
2 cups flour

2 tsp. baking powder
1/2 tsp. salt
1/2 tsp. ginger
1/4 tsp. baking soda
1/4 tsp. cloves
1/2 cup coarsely
   chopped walnuts

Cream together brown sugar and shortening till light and fluffy. Add eggs, one at a time, beating well after each addition. Stir in pumpkin and milk. Stir thoroughly the flour, baking powder, salt, ginger, baking soda and cloves; stir into pumpkin mixture. Beat 1 minute with electric or rotary beater. Stir in nuts. Turn into greased 9 x 5 x 3 inch loaf pan. Bake at 350° for 55 to 60 minutes. Remove from pan. Cool. Wrap and store overnight. Serve with butter.

Pumpkin Bread

1 large can pumpkin
2 1/2 cups honey
1 cup oil
2 eggs
2 1/2 cups whole wheat
  flour, sifted
2 1/2 cups unbleached
  flour, sifted

6 tsp. baking powder
4 tsp. cloves
1/2 tsp. salt
1 cup water
2 cups chopped nuts
2 cups raisins, optional

Mix together pumpkin, honey, oil and eggs. Add dry ingredients alternately with water. Add nuts and raisins. Bake 1 hour at 350° in 3 loaf pans.

Pumpkin-Pecan Bread

3 eggs
1 1/2 cups sugar
1 1/2 cup pumpkin
1 cup plus 2 Tbsp. salad
  oil
1 1/2 tsp. vanilla
2 1/4 cups flour
1 1/2 tsp. baking soda

1 1/2 tsp. baking powder
1 1/2 tsp. salt
1/4 tsp. cloves
1/4 tsp. nutmeg
1 1/2 tsp. cinnamon
1/4 tsp. ginger
3/4 cup chopped pecans

Beat eggs and sugar together well. Add pumpkin, oil and vanilla, mixing thoroughly. Sift flour, baking soda, baking powder, salt and spices. Add to pumpkin mixture and beat. Add pecans. Bake at 350° for 1 hour in 2 well greased loaf pans.

This freezes well. It is good sliced thin and spread with softened cream cheese for finger sandwiches.

Pumpkin Bread

1 cup sugar
1/4 cup salad oil
2 eggs, beaten
1 cup pumpkin
1 3/4 cups sifted flour
1 tsp. baking powder
1/2 tsp. baking soda
1/2 tsp. salt

1/2 tsp. each: cinnamon, nutmeg, allspice and cloves
1/2 cup raisins
1/3 cup water
1/2 cup chopped nuts, optional

Pour hot water over raisins; allow to cool. Add eggs to sugar, oil and pumpkin; beat well. Add dry ingredients; mix. Add raisins, water and nuts last. Mix well. Batter will be thin. Pour into 2 small loaf pans. Bake at 325° for 45-55 minutes.

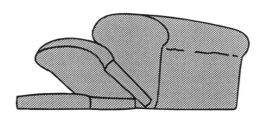

Pumpkin Bread

3 1/4 cups sifted flour
2 tsp. baking soda
2 cups sugar
1/2 tsp. salt
1 tsp. cinnamon
1 tsp. nutmeg
1/2 tsp. cloves, optional

1 cup oil
3 eggs, beaten
2 cups pumpkin
2/3 cup water
1 cup nuts or raisins, optional

Sift dry ingredients into large mixing bowl. Add remaining ingredients. Mix until smooth. Pour into 3 well-greased and floured loaf pans; bake at 350° for about 1 hour. Cool slightly in pans before turning out onto cooling racks.

Pumpkin Bread

3 cups sugar
1 cup oil
4 eggs, beaten
2 cups pumpkin
3 1/2 cups sifted flour
1 tsp. baking powder
2 tsp. baking soda
1/2 tsp. salt
1 1/2 tsp. pumpkin pie
   spice *or* 1 tsp. each:
   cinnamon, nutmeg
   and allspice
1/2 tsp. cloves, optional
1 tsp. cinnamon
2/3 cup water
1 cup pecans, optional

Combine sugar and oil; add beaten eggs, then add pumpkin. Add sifted dry ingredients and water. Mix; stir in nuts and pour into greased loaf pans or 1 pound coffee cans. Fill about 1/2 full. Bake at 350° for 55 minutes to 1 hour.

> *Pumpkin comes from the Greek word,*
> pepon, *meaning "a large melon."*

Pumpkin Yeast Rolls

1 pkg. dry yeast
1/4 cup lukewarm water
1 cup canned pumpkin
1 beaten egg
1/2 cup sugar
1/4 tsp. salt
1 Tbsp. butter
1 cup scalded milk
1 cup sifted flour

Mix yeast with water until dissolved. Add egg, sugar, salt, butter and milk to pumpkin. Add yeast and flour. Cover. Let rise in warm place overnight. Shape into biscuits. Let rise 20 minutes. Bake at 350° for 12-15 minutes. Makes 1 1/2 dozen biscuits.

Sorghum or molasses may be used instead of sugar with 3/4 cup milk instead of 1 cup.

Pumpkin Biscuits

2 cups flour
1/3 cup nonfat dry milk
1/4 cup sugar
2 tsp. baking powder
3/4 tsp. pumpkin pie spice

1/4 tsp. salt
1/2 cup shortening
3/4 cup pumpkin
1 Tbsp. water

Mix together flour, nonfat dry milk, sugar, baking powder, pumpkin pie spice and salt in medium bowl. Cut in shortening. Blend in pumpkin and water just until all ingredients are moistened. Knead 10-20 times on lightly floured surface. Using a 3 inch cookie cutter, cut into nine biscuits. Place biscuits on ungreased cookie sheet 2 inches apart. Bake in hot oven (400°) about 12-15 minutes or till golden brown.

Granny's Pumpkin Biscuits

3 cups flour
3 tsp. baking powder
1 tsp. salt
1 Tbsp. shortening

4 Tbsp. brown sugar
1 cup mashed, cooked
  pumpkin

Mix together the flour, salt and baking powder or use self-rising flour (eliminating salt and baking powder separately), cut in shortening. Add sugar and pumpkin; mix well. Roll or pat to 3/4 inch to 1 inch on floured board, cut with biscuit cutter and place on greased baking sheet. Bake at 425° for 20 minutes.

During the pumpkins' growth, vines spread along the ground, wrapping themselves around other parts of the plants to help the vines spread.

Basic Pumpkin Muffins

Stir thoroughly 1 1/2 cups flour, 1/2 cup sugar, 2 teaspoons baking powder, 3/4 teaspoon salt, 1/2 teaspoon cinnamon and 1/2 teaspoon nutmeg. Cut in 1/4 cup shortening till fine. Combine 1 beaten egg, 1/2 cup canned pumpkin and 1/2 cup milk; add to dry mixture and mix just till moistened. Stir in 1/2 cup light raisins. Fill greased muffin pans 2/3 full. Sprinkle additional sugar over each. Bake at 400° for 18-20 minutes. Makes 12 muffins.

Pumpkin Streusel Muffins

1 egg, beaten	**1/2 tsp. salt**
1/2 cup milk	**1/2 tsp. nutmeg**
1/2 cup canned pumpkin	**3 oz. pkg. cream cheese**
1/3 cup oil	
1 3/4 cups unbleached	**Streusel Topping:**
flour or all-purpose	**1/4 cup firmly packed**
flour	**brown sugar**
1/2 cup sugar	**1/2 tsp. cinnamon**
3 tsp. baking powder	**1 Tbsp. margarine**
1/2 to 1 tsp. cinnamon	**1/4 cup finely chopped**
	nuts

Heat oven to 400°. Line with paper baking cups or grease bottoms of 12 muffin cups. In medium bowl, combine egg, milk, pumpkin and oil; mix well; lightly spoon flour into measuring cup; level off. Stir in flour, sugar, baking powder, 1 teaspoon cinnamon, salt and nutmeg just until dry ingredients are moistened. (Batter will be lumpy). Fill prepared muffin cups about half full (reserve remaining batter). Divide cream cheese into 12 equal pieces. Place 1 piece on batter in each cup; top with reserved batter filling each cup about 3/4 full. Combine streusel topping ingredients, mix well. Sprinkle evenly over each muffin. Bake at 400° for 18 to 22 minutes or till golden brown. Serve warm.

Blueberry Streusel Muffins

1 2/3 cups flour
1 tsp. baking soda
1/2 tsp. baking powder
1 tsp. cinnamon
1/2 tsp. allspice
1/3 cup shortening
3/4 cup brown sugar
1 egg
1 cup pumpkin

1/4 cup evaporated milk
1 cup blueberries
1 Tbsp. flour

Streusel:
2 Tbsp. flour
2 Tbsp. sugar
1/4 tsp. cinnamon
1 Tbsp. butter

Combine first 5 ingredients. Cream shortening and sugar in large bowl. Add egg, beat until fluffy. Combine pumpkin and milk, blend well and add to creamed mixture alternately with flour mixture, mixing well after each addition. Combine blueberries with the tablespoon flour. Gently stir into batter. Fill muffin tins (greased and floured or lined with paper muffin cups) 3/4 full. Sprinkle with streusel mixture. For streusel, combine flour, sugar and cinnamon. Cut in butter until mixture is crumbly. Bake in 350° F. oven for 40 minutes or until done. (Test with toothpick.) Makes 1 1/2 dozen.

Pumpkin Nut Muffins

1 cup pumpkin
1/4 cup oil
2 eggs
1/4 cup milk
1 1/2 cups sugar

1/2 tsp. salt
1 tsp. baking soda
1 tsp. allspice
1 tsp. cinnamon

Blend above ingredients. Add:

1 3/4 cups flour
1/2 cup chopped nuts

Mix thoroughly. Put in greased muffin tins. Bake at 350° for 25 minutes. Makes 1 dozen.

Granny's Pumpkin Muffins

1 cup white seedless
  raisins
1/2 cup water
2 eggs
1 cup pumpkin
1 1/4 cups sugar
3/4 tsp. cinnamon
3/4 tsp. cloves
1/2 tsp. salt
1/3 cup vegetable oil
1 3/4 cups flour
1 1/2 tsp. baking powder
1/2 tsp. baking soda

Soak raisins in 1/2 cup water, set aside (do not drain). Combine eggs, pumpkin, sugar, spices, salt and oil, beat well. Stir in raisins and water, set aside. Combine remaining ingredients in large mixing bowl; make a well in center. Pour in pumpkin mixture, stirring just till moistened (batter will be lumpy). Spoon batter into greased muffin pans, filling 2/3 full. Bake at 400° for 25 minutes. Yield about 2 dozen muffins.

Pumpkin-Raisin Muffins
(Low Cholesterol)

2 eggs
1 cup honey
3/4 cup safflower oil
1 cup pumpkin
1 1/3 cups unbleached
  flour
1 tsp. baking powder
1 tsp. baking soda
1 tsp. cinnamon
1/2 tsp. allspice
dash salt
1/2 cup raisins
1/2 cup chopped nuts

Beat eggs well; add honey, oil and pumpkin. Add dry ingredients and mix well. Stir in raisins and nuts; fill paper-lined muffin cups 2/3 full. Bake 350° for 20 minutes.

Molasses Pumpkin Muffins

3/4 cup firmly packed
   brown sugar
1/2 cup margarine,
   softened
1/4 cup molasses
1 egg, beaten

1 cup canned pumpkin
1 3/4 cups flour
1 tsp. soda
1/4 tsp. salt
1/2 cup pecans or raisins

Combine sugar, margarine and molasses; beat well. Add egg and pumpkin beating until smooth. Stir together remaining ingredients; add to pumpkin mixture, stirring till just moistened (the batter will be lumpy). Fill lightly greased muffin pans half full. Bake at 350° for 20 minutes. Yield about 15 muffins.

Halloween Craft Project

Craft Dough Jack-o'-lantern

Mix together 2 cups of flour, 1 cup of salt and 1 cup of water. Knead into a dough of medium stiffness. Save aside some dough. Use paste food coloring to color the dough orange. Roll out the dough on flour-covered wax paper, forming a circle. Make a golf-sized ball from aluminum foil and place in the middle of the dough. Form the dough around the ball, pressing it to the foil at the top. Trim excess dough and form a "lid" to seal the pumpkin top. Smooth dough. Use cardboard patterns to press eyes and nose into the dough. Use toothpicks to make vertical pumpkin lines. Color remaining dough green for the stem. Press into place at top of pumpkin. Dry on a cookie sheet in a 325° oven for one to two hours. Cool, then dip into melted paraffin.

Cakes, Cookies and Bars

Pumpkin Cake

1 box yellow cake mix
1/2 cup oil
1/4 cup water
4 eggs

1 cup pumpkin or 16 oz. can
1 tsp. cinnamon
1 tsp. nutmeg
1/2 cup sugar

Mix and bake in tube pan at 350° for 1 hour.

Frosting for Pumpkin Cake

1 cup firmly packed
  brown sugar
1/2 cup white sugar
2 tsp. flour
1 cup milk

2 Tbsp. butter
1/2 cup pecans or
  walnuts
1 cup flaked coconut
1 tsp. vanilla

Combine first 4 ingredients. Cook over medium heat, stirring constantly until thickened (225° on candy thermometer). Add butter, stirring until melted. Stir in nuts, coconut and vanilla. Yield: enough for 1 (3 layer) cake.

Pumpkin Cake

2 cups sugar
1 1/2 sticks butter or
  margarine
3 eggs
2 cups pumpkin
1 tsp. vanilla

1 tsp. each: cloves,
  cinnamon, nutmeg
  and allspice
3 3/4 cups flour
1 1/2 tsp. baking powder
1/2 tsp. baking soda
1 1/2 cups chopped
  pecans

Cream sugar, butter and eggs, beat well. Add pumpkin, vanilla and dry ingredients, mix well. Add chopped nuts. Bake in a large tube pan for 1 hour at 350°.

> Pottery representing many varieties of pumpkins and squashes has been found by archaeologists throughout North and South America.

Pumpkin Pie Cake

1 (16 oz.) can pumpkin
3 eggs, beaten
3/4 cup sugar
3/4 cup brown sugar
2 tsp. pumpkin pie spice
1 (13 oz.) can
  evaporated milk

1 tsp. salt
1 (19 oz.) pkg. yellow
  cake mix
2 sticks butter, melted
1 cup broken pecans

Combine pumpkin, eggs, sugars, pie spice, milk and salt. Pour into an ungreased 9 x 13 inch pan. Spread dry cake mix over batter in pan. Pour butter evenly over cake mix; sprinkle with pecans. Bake at 350° for 1 hour and 15 minutes. Cool. Cut in squares.

Choco-Dot Pumpkin Cake

4 eggs
1 can pumpkin (2 cup)
1 cup vegetable oil
1 cup All-Bran (or 1 1/2
  cup Bran Flakes)
1 1/2 cups sugar
2 cups flour
2 tsp. baking powder

1 tsp. baking soda
1 1/2 tsp. cinnamon
1/2 tsp. ground cloves
1/4 tsp. allspice
1/4 tsp. ginger
1 cup chocolate chips
1 cup coarsely chopped
  nuts

In large bowl, beat eggs until foamy. Add pumpkin, oil and bran. Mix well. Add sifted dry ingredients, mixing only until combined. Stir in chocolate bits and nuts. Spread evenly in 10 x 4 inch tube pan (angel food pan) ungreased or sprayed lightly with Pam. Bake at 350° for about 1 hour and 10 minutes or until cake tests done with a toothpick inserted near center. Cool completely before removing from pan. (May need to place a sheet of foil across top during last 1/2 hour to avoid over-browning.) Serves 16.

Pumpkin Pie-Cake

4 eggs, slightly beaten
1 can (16 or 20 oz.)
  pumpkin
1 1/2 cups sugar
2 tsp. pumpkin pie spice
1 tsp. salt

1 can (13 oz.)
  evaporated milk
1 (18 oz.) yellow cake mix
1 cup margarine, melted
1 cup chopped pecans

Mix first 6 ingredients in order listed; pour into 9 x 13 inch or 11 x 15 inch pan. Sprinkle cake mix over filling. Pour melted butter over top of cake; sprinkle with pecans. Bake at 350° for 1 - 1 1/2 hours or till knife comes out clean when inserted halfway from center. (With 11 x 15 inch pan, temperature may be set at 375° and bake 35 to 45 minutes.) Serve warm or chilled, plain or with whipped topping.

Pumpkin-Spice Cake

2 1/4 cups sifted cake
  flour
1 Tbsp. baking powder
1 1/2 tsp. cinnamon
3/4 tsp. cloves
3/4 tsp. nutmeg
7 eggs, separated
1/2 tsp. cream of tartar
1/2 of a 16 oz. can (1
  cup) pumpkin

1/2 cup cooking oil
non-calorie liquid sweet-
  ener equal to 1/2 cup
  sugar
1/2 tsp. finely shredded
  orange peel
1-1 1/4 oz. envelope
  low-calorie dessert
  topping mix, whipped

Stir together flour, baking powder, spices and 1/4 tea-spoon salt. Add egg yolks, pumpkin, oil, sweetener and peel; beat till smooth. Beat egg whites with cream of tartar till stiff peaks form. Fold 1/3 of the whites into batter; fold batter into remaining 2/3 of whites. Bake in ungreased 9 inch tube pan in 325° oven for 60 minutes. Invert cake in pan. Cool. Serve with whipped topping. Makes 16 servings.

Pumpkin Layer Cake

1 1/2 cups sugar
4 eggs, well beaten
1 cup corn oil
1 tsp. vanilla
2 cups pumpkin

2 cups flour
1 tsp. baking soda
1 tsp. baking powder
1 tsp. cinnamon
1 tsp. allspice

Combine sugar, eggs, oil, vanilla and pumpkin; mix well. Add dry ingredients; beat 1 minute at medium speed of electric mixer. Pour into 3 greased and floured 9 inch round cake pans. Bake at 325° for 25-30 minutes or until done. Cool in pans 10 minutes. Remove from pans. Allow to cool completely. Spread frosting between layers and on top. For easier slicing, chill in refrigerator. (Can also be baked in a 9 x 13 inch pan.) Frost with frosting for Pumpkin Cake.

Natural Foods Bundt Cake

1 cup safflower oil
3 eggs
2 cups canned pumpkin
2 cups fructose
1/4 cup honey
1/4 cup soy flour
1/4 cup nutritional yeast
2 1/4 cups unbleached
  flour

2 tsp. baking powder
1/2 tsp. baking soda
1 tsp. cinnamon
1 tsp. allspice
1/2 tsp. ginger
1/2 tsp. cloves
1 cup nuts, chopped
1 cup raisins

Beat oil, eggs, pumpkin, fructose and honey until well mixed. Add dry ingredients and beat on medium speed for 1 minute. Stir in raisins and nuts; turn into greased and floured Bundt pan. Bake 1 hour at 350°; cool 15 minutes and invert.

Hint: be sure cake is completely cooled before you invert.

Scrumptious Pumpkin Cake

Blend on high for 1 minute till thoroughly mixed:

1/2 cup oil
3 eggs
2 cups pumpkin

1/3 cup sugar
1/2 cup milk

Add box of **chocolate cake mix**. Mix on high for 2 minutes. Stir in **1 cup mini chocolate chips** and **1 cup chopped pecans.** Grease and flour jelly roll pan. Pour mixture in pan. Bake at 350° for 25-30 minutes or until toothpick comes out clean.

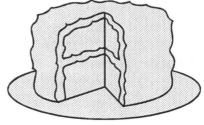

Frost with fudge icing if desired or sprinkle with confectioners sugar. Refrigerate leftovers. Tastes even better next day.

Pumpkin Date Cake

1/2 cup chopped dates
1/2 cup chopped walnuts
2 Tbsp. flour
1/4 cup butter
1 cup firmly packed
   brown sugar
2/3 cup pumpkin
1 tsp. vanilla
2 eggs

1/2 tsp. cinnamon
1/4 tsp. ginger
1/2 cup flour
1/2 tsp. baking powder
1/4 tsp. baking soda
1/2 tsp. nutmeg
whipped cream
date halves, optional

Combine chopped dates, walnuts and 2 tablespoons flour, mix well. Set aside. Melt butter over low heat; stir in brown sugar. Remove from heat; stir in pumpkin and vanilla. Add eggs, one at a time, beating well after each addition. Combine remaining dry ingredients; add to pumpkin mixture, mixing well. Stir in floured date mixture. Pour into greased 8 inch square pan. Bake at 350° about 30 minutes. Serve warm. Top each serving with whipped cream, garnish with a date half, if desired.

Pumpkin Cake

1/2 cup shortening
1 1/2 cup sugar
3/4 cup milk
2 eggs
2 cups flour
1 tsp. soda

2 tsp. baking powder
1/2 tsp. each: cinnamon,
   ginger, nutmeg, salt
   and vanilla
1 cup pumpkin
1 cup nut meats

Cream shortening, sugar. Stir in milk. Add eggs, beating well. Mix dry ingredients. Add pumpkin alternately with dry ingredients to creamed mixture. Stir in nuts. Bake at 350° about 40 minutes.

Basic Pumpkin Cake

4 eggs
1 2/3 cups sugar
1 cup cooking oil
1 (16 oz.) can pumpkin
2 cups flour

2 tsp. baking powder
2 tsp. cinnamon
1 tsp. salt
1 tsp. baking soda
Cream Cheese icing

In large mixing bowl, beat together eggs, sugar, oil and pumpkin until light and fluffy. Stir together flour, baking powder, cinnamon, salt and baking soda. Add to pumpkin mixture and mix thoroughly. Spread batter in ungreased baking pan. Bake in preheated 350° oven for 25 to 30 minutes. Cool. Frost with your favorite cream cheese frosting recipe.

Pumpkin Buttermilk Cake

1/2 cup shortening
1 cup brown sugar

1/2 cup granulated sugar

Cream well. Add:

2 beaten eggs
3/4 cup mashed pumpkin

Stir in:

2 cups all-purpose flour
1 tsp. baking powder
1/2 tsp. baking soda
1 tsp. salt

1/2 tsp. cinnamon
1/2 tsp. nutmeg
1/2 tsp. allspice
1/2 cup buttermilk

Sift dry ingredients together and add alternately with buttermilk. Stir in:

3/4 cup English walnuts
or pecans, chopped

Turn into greased and floured 8 inch layer cake pans. 350° oven for 25-30 minutes.

Pumpkin Cake

2 cups sugar
1 (16 oz.) can pumpkin
1 cup vegetable oil
4 eggs, beaten
2 cups flour
1 tsp. salt

2 tsp. baking soda
2 tsp. baking powder
2 tsp. cinnamon
1/2 cup flaked coconut
1/2 cup chopped pecans
frosting

Combine sugar, pumpkin, oil and eggs; beat 1 minute at medium speed of electric mixer. Combine next 5 ingredients; add to pumpkin mixture. Beat 1 minute, at medium speed. Stir in coconut and pecans. Pour batter into 3 greased and floured 8 inch round cake pans. Bake at 350° for 25 to 30 or till cake tests done. Cool in pans 10 minutes. Remove from pans and cool completely. Spread frosting between layers and on top of cake.

Frosting:

1/2 cup margarine
1 (8 oz.) pkg. cream
  cheese, softened
1 (16 oz.) pkg. powdered
  sugar

2 tsp. vanilla
1/2 cup chopped pecans
1/2 cup flaked coconut

Combine margarine and cream cheese; beat till light and fluffy. Add sugar and vanilla, mixing well. Stir in pecans and coconut.

*For Halloween decorating,
make a pumpkin totem pole. Carve
three pumpkins into jack-o'-lanterns,
then stack on top of one another
(largest on the bottom). Use pieces
of dowel rod to join
them together.*

Spicy Pumpkin Sheet Cake

(15 x 10 inch cake)
4 eggs
1 3/4 cups (16 oz.)
  pumpkin
1 cup sugar
3/4 cup firmly packed
  brown sugar
1 cup oil

1/2 tsp. ginger
1/2 tsp. salt
2 cups flour
2 tsp. baking powder
1 tsp. soda
1 tsp. cinnamon
1/2 tsp. nutmeg
cream cheese frosting

Beat eggs in large mixer bowl. Add pumpkin, sugars and oil, beat well. Add remaining ingredients except frosting. Beat until well blended. Spread into greased 15 x 10 x 1 inch jelly roll pan. Bake at 350° for 25 minutes or till toothpick inserted in center comes out clean. Cool. Frost with Cream Cheese Frosting.

Cream Cheese Frosting

Combine:

3 oz. cream cheese
1 tsp. vanilla

1/4 cup butter
2 cups powdered sugar

Beat in small mixer bowl till light and fluffy.

Decorations for Halloween

Crescent Moon–Use crescent shaped cookie cutter. Press lightly onto top of cake to leave an outline. Fill outline with frosting.

Bats–Draw bats using black frosting in a pastry bag with a fine tip.

Fence and Tombstones Frosting for Pumpkin Sheet Cake–Frost graham crackers with white frosting. Cut in strips to make picket fence. Use a dab of frosting to hold fence together and fasten graham crackers to side of fence. Cut 1/4 graham cracker to look like tombstone. For gray marble tombstone appearance, frost with black frosting. Wipe off excess with spatula and cover with white frosting. Using pastry bag with fine tip, write R.I.P. in black frosting. To stand tombstones, cut a small slash in top of cake in which you insert the tombstone. Place a dab of frosting in back of tombstone. Lean back to brace.

Pumpkin Cup Cakes

1/2 cup shortening
1 1/2 cups sugar
2 eggs, beaten
2 1/2 tsp. baking powder
1 tsp. salt
2 1/4 cups all-purpose
   flour

1/2 tsp. baking soda
2 tsp. cinnamon
1/2 tsp. nutmeg
1/2 tsp. ginger
1 cup pumpkin cooked
3/4 cup milk
1/2 cup nuts

Cream shortening, add sugar, blend in beaten eggs. Sift flour, baking powder, baking soda, salt and spices together. Combine pumpkin and milk. Add dry ingredients alternately with pumpkin mixture. Stir in chopped nuts, pour batter into 24 wax paper cups. Bake in muffin tins to hold shape. Bake for 25 minutes at 350°. Cool. Cover with butter cream icing, flavored with grated orange rind.

Pumpkin Roll

3 eggs
3/4 cup sugar
3/4 cup flour
1 tsp. baking powder
2 tsp. ginger

1/2 tsp. nutmeg
2/3 cup canned pumpkin
1 tsp. lemon juice
1 cup chopped pecans

Beat eggs at high speed for 5 minutes. Gradually beat in sugar. Stir in pumpkin and lemon juice. Sift dry ingredients together (flour, baking powder and spices) and fold–do not beat–into pumpkin. Spread in a greased and floured 15 x 10 x 1 inch pan. Top with finely chopped nuts. Bake at 375° for 15 minutes. Turn out onto towel sprinkled with powdered sugar. Starting at one end, roll towel and cake together. Cool before unrolling. Remove from towel, spread with filling, reroll and chill.

Filling:

1 cup powdered sugar
2 (3 oz.) pkgs. cream
cheese

4 Tbsp. margarine
1/2 tsp. vanilla

Combine powdered sugar, cream cheese, butter and vanilla. Beat until SMOOTH.

Native American Indians were growing pumpkins for hundreds of years before Europeans first came to America. They grew them in mounds among their other crops. They used pumpkin chunks in stew and fed pumpkin pieces to their horses.

Pumpkin Roll

3 eggs	1 tsp. baking powder
1 cup sugar	2 tsp. cinnamon
3/4 cup pumpkin	1 tsp. ginger
3/4 cup flour	1/2 tsp. nutmeg

Beat eggs for 5 minutes on high speed. Beat in sugar. Stir in pumpkin, flour, baking powder and spices. Pour into greased and floured 11 x 15 inch pan (cookie sheet). Bake at 375° for 15 minutes. Prepare a towel–sprinkle generously with powdered sugar. Remove cake from oven and turn out onto towel. Cut off edges and roll up, starting with the end (a short side). Refrigerate to cool.

Filling:

1 cup powdered sugar	4 Tbsp. butter
3 oz. softened cream	1/2 tsp. vanilla
cheese	1 cup chopped pecans

Beat together and spread on unrolled cake. Reroll and chill.

How to roast pumpkin seeds

Wash the seeds in cold water then blot them on a paper towel. Preheat oven to 250°. Spread seeds evenly in a single layer on a cookie sheet, sprinkle with salt and roast for 30 to 60 minutes. Check the seeds frequently; they are done when dry and light brown. Cool.

Pumpkin Roll With Cream Cheese Filling

Beat **3 eggs** for 5 minutes. Add:

1 cup sugar	**1 tsp. ginger**
1/3 cup pumpkin	**1/2 tsp. nutmeg**
1 tsp. lemon juice	**3/4 cup flour**
2 tsp. cinnamon	

Spread on 15 x 10 inch cookie sheet. Top with 1/2 cup nuts. Bake at 375° for 15 minutes. Take up on floured tea towel (powdered sugar). Roll up and chill.

Filling:

1 cup powdered sugar	**4 Tbsp. butter**
6 oz. cream cheese	**1/2 tsp. vanilla**

Blend well. Unroll and spread filling. Roll up again. Chill. Slice.

Pumpkin Cake Roll

3 eggs
1 cup sugar
2/3 cup pumpkin
1 tsp. lemon juice
3/4 cup flour
1 tsp. baking powder
1/2 tsp. salt
2 tsp. cinnamon
1 tsp. ginger

1/2 tsp. nutmeg
1 cup walnuts

Filling:
1/4 cup butter
3 (3 oz.) pkgs. cream
    cheese
1/2 tsp. vanilla
1 cup powdered sugar

Mix eggs until lemon colored. While mixing, add sugar gradually, mix until slightly thickened. Add the pumpkin and lemon juice; add sifted flour, baking powder, salt and spices, mix until flour disappears, don't overmix. Spread batter in greased and floured 15 x 10 x 1 inch pan. Sprinkle with chopped walnuts. Bake at 375° for 15 minutes. Turn out on towel sprinkled with powdered sugar. Starting at narrow end, roll up cake and towel together, nuts on outside of roll. Cool on rack.

Filling:

Cream butter, cream cheese and vanilla; add 1 cup powdered sugar. Mix until smooth; spread on unrolled cake. Reroll; chill at least 2 hours. Slice to serve.

At the pumpkin festival in Sycamore, Illinois, five tons of pumpkins are donated to the townsfolk for carving into scupltures and jack-o'-lanterns. They are exhibited on the lawn of the De Kalb County Courthouse.

Pumpkin Log

3 eggs
2/3 cup pumpkin
1 cup sugar

1 tsp. baking soda
1/2 tsp. cinnamon
3/4 cup flour
1/2 cup chopped nuts

Filling:

2 Tbsp. butter
8 oz. cream cheese

3/4 tsp. vanilla
1 cup sugar

Grease 10 x 15 1/2 inch cookie sheet, place waxed paper on sheet and grease again. Mix first ingredients and pour in prepared pan. Sprinkle with 1/2 cup chopped nuts. Bake at 375° for 15 minutes. Turn on well-sugared towel immediately, remove wax paper and roll like jelly roll with towel. Cool 1 hour on rack. Then unroll and fill.

Mix together ingredients for filling and spread on cooled cake. Roll back up. Refrigerate. Slice. Serve and enjoy!

Pumpkin Cake Icing:

1 cup Crisco
1 cup brown sugar
2 Tbsp. powdered sugar

1 egg
1 Tbsp. vanilla
1/4 cup canned milk

Mix in bowl and beat until creamy.

Maple Pumpkin Cheesecake

1 1/4 cups graham cracker crumbs
1/4 cup sugar
1/4 cup margarine, melted
3 (8 oz.) pkgs. cream cheese, softened
1 (14 oz.) can Eagle Brand sweetened condensed milk
1 (16 oz.) can pumpkin (2 cup)
3 eggs
1 cup Vermont Maple Orchards or MacDonalds pure maple syrup
1 1/2 tsp. cinnamon
1 tsp. nutmeg
1/2 tsp. salt
maple pecan glaze

Preheat oven to 300°. Combine crumbs, sugar and margarine, press firmly on bottom of 9 inch spring form pan or 13 x 9 inch baking pan. In large bowl, beat cheese till fluffy. Gradually add milk till smooth. Add pumpkin, eggs, 1/4 cup maple syrup, cinnamon, nutmeg and salt. Mix well. Pour into prepared pan. Bake 1 hour and 15 minutes or until edge springs back when lightly touched (center will be slightly soft). Cool. Chill. Top with Maple Pecan Glaze. Refrigerate leftovers.

Maple Pecan Glaze

In pan, combine remaining 3/4 cup maple syrup, 1 cup (1/2 pint) whipping cream, unwhipped; bring to a boil. Boil rapidly 15-20 minutes or till thickened, stir occasionally. Add 1/2 cup chopped pecans.

Pumpkin seeds sprout in eight to 10 days. Two seed leaves are the first to appear. They nourish the plant until true pumpkin leaves develop.

Pumpkin Cheesecake

1 1/2 cups zwieback crumbs
3 Tbsp. sugar
3 Tbsp. melted butter or
margarine
2 (8 oz.) pkgs. cream
cheese, softened
1 cup light cream
1 cup canned pumpkin
3/4 cup sugar

4 eggs, separated
3 Tbsp. flour
1 tsp. vanilla
1 tsp. cinnamon
1/2 tsp. ginger
1 1/2 tsp. nutmeg
1 cup sour cream
2 Tbsp. sugar
1/2 tsp. vanilla

Combine first 3 ingredients, press into bottom and 2 inches up sides of 9 inch spring form pan. Bake at 325° for 5 minutes. In large mixing bowl, combine cream cheese, cream, pumpkin, sugar, egg yolks, flour, vanilla and spices. Beat till smooth, folding in the 4 stiffly beaten egg whites. Turn into prepared crust. Bake at 325° for 1 hour. Combine sour cream, the 2 tablespoons sugar and 1/2 teaspoon vanilla. Spread over cheesecake. Bake for another 5 minutes. Cool thoroughly before serving.

Pumpkin Cheesecake

1/2 cup vanilla wafer crumbs
1 Tbsp. melted butter
2 cup dry cottage cheese
3 egg yolks
1 cup canned pumpkin
1/4 cup reconstituted
nonfat dry milk

1/2 cup sugar
1 tsp. vanilla
1/2 tsp. cinnamon
1/4 tsp. ground ginger
dash cloves
1/4 tsp. ground nutmeg
3 stiffly beaten egg whites

Combine wafer crumbs and melted butter. Press in bottom of spring form 8 inch pan. Bake 325° for 8-10 minutes. Cool. Press cottage cheese through sieve. Beat in egg yolks, pumpkin, milk, sugar, vanilla and spices. Beat till smooth. Fold in stiffly beaten egg whites. Spoon into crust. Bake at 325° until set, 25 minutes. Chill. 12 servings.

Pumpkin Cheesecake

(Low calorie, low fat)

nonstick vegetable
  cooking spray
3 Tbsp. finely crushed
  zwieback biscuit
  crumbs
1 1/2 cups low fat
  cottage cheese
1 1/2 cups canned
  pumpkin puree
1/2 cup sugar

1/4 cup firmly packed
  dark brown sugar
3 Tbsp. flour
2 eggs, slightly beaten
3/4 cup skim milk
1/2 tsp. salt
2 tsp. fresh lemon juice
1/8 tsp. nutmeg
1/2 tsp. ginger
1 tsp. cinnamon

Preheat oven to 350°. Spray cooking spray on inside of 8 inch spring form pan with tight-fitting bottom. Sprinkle the pan with biscuit crumbs. Place the cottage cheese in food processor. Whirl until cheese is very smooth (there should be no lumps) scraping down the side of the container. Add the pumpkin puree, granulated and brown sugars, flour, eggs, milk, lemon juice, cinnamon, ginger, salt and nutmeg to the processor. Whirl until the cheese mixture is smooth. Let stand in processor 5 minutes. Ladle cheese mixture into the prepared pan. Bake in preheated oven 350° for 45 minutes; the outer edge will be set but center still will be soft. Turn off oven. Let cake stay in oven for 30 minutes. Cool cake slightly in the pan on a wire rack. Refrigerate the cake in the pan, lightly covered, overnight, or until cake is well chilled. To serve, run a sharp knife around the outer edge of the cake and remove the pan side.

Pumpkins are 90 percent water.

Pumpkin Cookies

1/2 cup shortening
1 cup white sugar
1/2 cup brown sugar
2 eggs
1 1/2 cups pumpkin
1 tsp. lemon juice
2 1/2 cups flour
1/4 tsp. ginger
2 tsp. baking powder
1/2 tsp. baking soda

1 tsp. cinnamon
1/2 tsp. nutmeg
1 cup chopped nuts
1 cup raisins

Glaze:
2 Tbsp. butter
2 cups powdered sugar
2 Tbsp. lemon juice
2 Tbsp. hot milk

Cream shortening, sugars and eggs together. Blend in pumpkin and lemon juice. Add sifted dry ingredients, nuts and raisins and mix together. Drop by teaspoons on greased cookie sheet. (Cookies will puff up.) Bake 12-15 minutes at 375°. Combine glaze ingredients for *cooled* cookies.

Chocolate Chip Drop Cookies

1/2 cup margarine,
  softened
1 cup firmly packed
  brown sugar
3/4 cup sugar
1 cup pumpkin
1 egg
1 tsp. cinnamon
1/2 tsp. nutmeg
1 1/4 cups flour

1 1/2 tsp. salt
1 tsp. baking powder
1/4 tsp. baking soda
3/4 cup quick-cooking
  oats, uncooked
1 cup raisins
1 cup chopped pecans or
  black walnuts
1 (6 oz.) pkg. semi-sweet
  chocolate morsels

Combine margarine and sugar, creaming thoroughly. Add pumpkin, egg, cinnamon and nutmeg; beat mixture until light and fluffy. Add flour, salt, baking powder and baking soda, mixing well. Stir in remaining ingredients. Drop by teaspoonfuls onto lightly greased cookie sheets. Bake at 375° for 12 to 15 minutes. Cool on rack. Makes 6 dozen cookies.

Maine Pumpkin Cookies with Frosting

1/2 cup granulated sugar	1 1/2 cups sifted flour
1/2 cup firmly packed brown sugar	1 tsp. baking powder
1/2 cup shortening	1/2 tsp. baking soda
2 eggs	1 tsp. vanilla
1 cup canned or cooked and strained pumpkin	1 cup candied fruit
	1/2 cup chopped nuts

Cream sugars and shortening together. Add eggs, beat well. Add pumpkin, then sifted dry ingredients. Mix well. Add vanilla, candied fruit and nuts. Drop by spoonful onto greased cookie sheets. Bake at 350° for 10-12 minutes. Remove from pans. Cool, then frost. Makes 3 dozen medium size cookies.

Frosting

1/4 cup light brown sugar	1 tsp. vanilla
1/4 cup butter or margarine (1/2 stick)	1 cup confectioners sugar

Mix margarine or butter and brown sugar in saucepan. Cook over low heat for about 10 minutes. Add confectioners sugar and vanilla. Mix well and spread on cookies. (If frosting is too thick, add a bit of cream or milk before spreading.)

Pumpkins grow faster when fed with milk or sugar water through a slit in their stalks. Some double their size in only a few days.

Brown Sugar Frosted Cookies

1 cup butter
1 cup sugar
1 cup pumpkin
1 egg
1 tsp. vanilla
2 cups flour
1 tsp. baking powder

1 tsp. baking soda
1 tsp. cinnamon
1/2 tsp. salt
1/2 cup chopped dates
  or raisins
1/2 cup chopped nuts

Cream together butter and sugar. Add next 3 ingredients and mix well. Sift dry ingredients and blend into creamed mixture. Stir in dates or raisins and nuts. Drop onto greased cookie sheet. Bake at 375° for 10 to 15 minutes. Cool on racks and prepare icing.

Icing

1/2 cup brown sugar
1/4 cup milk
3 Tbsp. butter

3/4 tsp. vanilla
1 cup powdered sugar

In a saucepan, combine brown sugar, milk and butter. Cook 2 minutes. Remove from heat. Let cool. Stir in vanilla and powdered sugar. Makes 4 to 5 dozen.

Pumpkins are from the horticultural family, Cucurbitaceae, along with squashes, melons, cucumbers and gourds. Of the 700 species, some are raised for fruits, while others are used for ornaments, utensils and sponges.

Refrigerator Pumpkin Cookies

1 cup butter, softened
2 cups sugar
1 cup pumpkin
3 cups flour

1 Tbsp. pumpkin pie
  spice
1/2 tsp. salt

Cream butter, gradually add sugar, beating till light and fluffy. Alternate additions of pumpkin and combined dry ingredients, mixing well after each addition. Cover; chill until dough is firm. Divide dough into 4 parts. Place each part on a 14 x 10 inch sheet of plastic wrap. Wrap plastic loosely around dough; shape into a 10 x 1 1/2 inch roll. Wrap securely. Freeze at least 4 hours. Dough may be frozen up to 4 months. To bake, unwrap rolls. Cut into 1/8 inch slices. Place on lightly greased cookie sheets about 1/2 inch apart. Sprinkle with mixture of 2 tablespoons sugar and 1/2 teaspoon pumpkin pie spice. Bake in preheated 350° oven 16 to 18 minutes or till lightly browned. Remove from cookie sheets. Cool on wire racks.

Frosted Pumpkin Cookies

1/2 cup butter
1/2 cup sugar
1 1/2 cups brown sugar
1 tsp. vanilla
2 eggs
1 Tbsp. lemon juice
2 1/2 cups flour
3/4 tsp. soda

2 tsp. baking powder
1/2 tsp. salt
1 tsp. ginger
1 tsp. cinnamon
1 1/2 cups pumpkin
1/2 cup raisins
1/2 cup nuts

Combine butter, sugars, vanilla, eggs and lemon juice. Add dry ingredients, alternately with pumpkin. Stir in raisins and nuts. Drop by teaspoonfuls onto lightly greased cookie sheet. Bake at 350° for 15 minutes. Yield 3 1/2 dozen.

Frosting

1 egg, beaten
4 Tbsp. butter
1 tsp. lemon juice

1/4 cup pumpkin
3 cups powdered sugar

Heat egg, butter, lemon juice and pumpkin. Add powdered sugar. Spread on cooled cookies.

Colonists preserved pumpkins by drying them. They were sliced and placed on racks in the sun or hung from the rafters until they were dry.

Pumpkin Drop Cookies

2 1/4 cups unsifted flour
2 tsp. baking powder
1 tsp. cinnamon
1 tsp. allspice
1/4 tsp. ginger
1/2 tsp. salt
1/3 cup shortening
1 cup sugar
1 cup pumpkin
2 eggs
1 tsp. lemon juice
1 tsp. vanilla
1/2 cup flaked coconut
1 cup raisins
1/2 cup chopped walnuts

Sift together flour, baking powder, spices and salt, set aside. Cream together shortening and sugar in bowl till light and fluffy, using electric mixer at medium speed. Beat in pumpkin, eggs, lemon juice and vanilla, blend well. Gradually stir dry ingredients into creamed mixture, mixing well. Stir in raisins, coconut and walnuts. Drop mixture by heaping teaspoonfuls about 2 inches apart on greased baking sheets. Bake in 350° oven for 10-12 minutes or till golden brown. Remove from baking sheets; cool on racks. Makes 4 dozen.

The pumpkin is a model of ecological efficiency. The "meat" can be used to prepare a variety of delicious, healthful foods. The seeds can be roasted and eaten. The shell can be used for a jack-o'-lantern, a scarecrow's head or an autumn table centerpiece. And when its productive life is over, the pumpkin makes excellent compost material.

Harvest Pumpkin Cookies

1 cup flour
1/2 cup quick oats
1/2 cup shredded
coconut
2 Tbsp. wheat germ
1/2 tsp. baking soda
1/2 tsp. cinnamon
1/4 tsp. salt
1/2 cup softened butter

1/2 cup firmly packed
brown sugar
1/2 cup sugar
1 egg
1 tsp. vanilla
3/4 cup pumpkin
1/2 cup chopped nuts
1/2 cup raisins

Combine flour, oats, coconut, wheat germ, baking soda, cinnamon and salt. Cream butter and sugars in large mixer bowl. Add egg and vanilla, beat till fluffy. Add dry ingredients alternately with pumpkin, beating well after each addition. Stir in raisins and nuts. Drop by rounded tablespoon onto lightly greased cookie sheet. Spread with metal spatula to 3/8 inch thickness. Bake in 350° oven for 15 to 20 minutes or till lightly browned. Cool on racks. Makes 2 dozen.

Date-Nut Pumpkin Cookies

1 cup butter or
  margarine
1/2 cup light brown
  sugar, firmly packed
1/2 cup sugar
1 egg
1 cup pumpkin
1 tsp. vanilla

2 cups sifted flour
1 tsp. baking powder
1 tsp. soda
1 tsp. cinnamon
1/2 tsp. salt
1 cup snipped dates
1 cup chopped walnuts

Preheat oven to 350°. In large bowl, beat butter and sugars together until fluffy. Add pumpkin, egg and vanilla, mix well. Sift dry ingredients and spices together. Add to pumpkin mixture and stir to mix well. Stir in nuts and dates. Drop batter by heaping teaspoonfuls onto ungreased baking sheets, 1 inch apart. Bake at 350° for 15 minutes or until tops are golden and centers firm to the touch. Remove from baking sheets and cool on wire racks. Makes 4 dozen.

Pumpkin was nearly a daily staple for colonists in the New World. It was sliced and roasted, baked whole (after removing the seeds), boiled and made into dough for pancakes.

Pumpkin Owl Cookies

4 cups flour
1 cup oats, uncooked
1 tsp. baking soda
1 tsp. cinnamon
1/2 tsp. salt
1 cup margarine,
softened
1 cup firmly packed
brown sugar
1 cup sugar

1 egg
1 tsp. vanilla
1 cup pumpkin
1 cup semi-sweet choco-
late morsels
1 large Brazil nut,
cashew or almond
string licorice, if desired
packaged chocolate and
white frosting

Combine flour, oats, baking soda, cinnamon and salt; set aside. Cream margarine; gradually add sugars, beating till light and fluffy. Add egg and vanilla; mix well. Alternate additions of dry ingredients and pumpkin, mixing well after each addition. Stir in morsels. Chill dough. Place half of dough in a non-stick or greased and floured 15 1/2 x 10 1/2 inch pan, spread into owl shape (about 13 1/2 inches high and 8 1/2 inch wide) using thin metal spatula. Use remaining dough to form branch (3/4 to 1 cup) and extra cookies on a cookie sheet, or make second owl. Bake in preheated 350° oven 20 to 25 minutes or till wooden toothpick inserted near center comes out clean. Cool pan on wire rack. Decorate using frostings and nut for owl beak. Licorice or chocolate frosting can be used to make owl's claws. Makes 2 owls or 1 owl, branch and 4 cookies.

Pumpkin Pinwheel Ice Cream Cookie Sandwich

2 cups (16 oz.) pureed
  pumpkin
3 cups sugar
1 tsp. pumpkin pie spice
1 cup chopped nuts
3 eggs

1/2 tsp. salt
1 cup shortening
4 cups flour
1/2 tsp. baking soda
1/2 tsp. cinnamon

Combine pumpkin, 1 cup sugar and pie spice in pan. Heat to boiling. Reduce heat, simmer 10 minutes. Stir in nuts; cool and reserve. Cream shortening and remaining 2 cups sugar in large mixer bowl. Add eggs; beat till fluffy. Combine remaining ingredients. Add to creamed mixture. Mix well. Divide dough into 3 equal parts. On lightly floured foil, roll each into an 8 x 12 inch rectangle. Spread with 1/3 of reserved filling mixture. Starting from wide end, roll as for jelly roll. Wrap in foil. Repeat with remaining dough and filling. Place rolls in freezer several hours or overnight. To bake, remove 1 roll at a time from freezer; unwrap and cut with sharp knife into 3/8 inch slices. Arrange on greased cookie sheets. Bake at 400° for 10 to 12 minutes. Cool. Insert about 1/4 cup of vanilla or pumpkin ice cream between 2 cookies. Keep frozen.

Young pumpkin buds on long stems become male flowers. Female buds on short stems sit atop green bulbous ovaries that will become pumpkins when they are pollinated.

Easy Pumpkin Bars

2 cups sugar
1/2 cup oil
16 oz. can pumpkin
4 eggs, beaten

2 cups Bisquick
2 tsp. cinnamon
1/2 cup raisins, optional

Grease jelly roll pan. Beat sugar, oil, pumpkin and eggs for 1 minute. Stir in Bisquick, cinnamon and raisins. Pour into pan and bake until toothpick comes out clean in center. Cool and then frost and refrigerate.

Cream Cheese Frosting

3 oz. cream cheese,
softened
1 Tbsp. milk

1/3 cup margarine,
softened
1 tsp. vanilla
2 cups powdered sugar

Beat until creamy, then add 2 cups powdered sugar. Bake cake at 350° for 30 minutes before frosting.

Pumpkin Bars

1/4 lb. margarine
1 egg
1 cup brown sugar
1/2 cup pumpkin
1 1/2 cup flour
1 tsp. cinnamon

1/2 tsp. ginger
1/2 tsp. allspice
1/2 tsp. baking soda
1/2 cup raisins
1/2 cup nuts

Mix ingredients together. Bake in 9 x 13 inch (or slightly smaller) pan at 350° about 30 minutes.

Glaze

1 cup powdered sugar
3 tsp. orange juice

1 tsp. orange rind

Mix together and spread on while warm.

Pumpkin Bars

2 cups sugar
4 eggs
2 cups flour
2 tsp. baking powder
1 tsp. soda

2 cups (1 can) pumpkin
1 cup oil
1 tsp. cinnamon
1 tsp. vanilla
nuts, optional

Mix together. Bake at 325° for 25 minutes. Cool.

Icing

3 oz. pkg. cream cheese
3/4 stick margarine
1 tsp. vanilla

1-3 Tbsp. milk
2-3 cups sugar

Let cream cheese and margarine be at room temperature; mix all ingredients together. Frost when bars are cool.

Easy Frosted Pumpkin Bars

1/3 cup sugar
1/3 cup oil
3 eggs
15 oz. can pumpkin
1 pkg. butter recipe cake
mix

3 tsp. pumpkin pie spice
1 can ready-to-spread
vanilla frosting
3 oz. pkg. cream cheese,
softened

Heat oven to 350°. Grease and flour 15 x 10 inch jelly roll pan. In large bowl, combine sugar, oil, eggs and pumpkin; beat 1 minute at highest speed. Add cake mix and spice, blend till moistened. Beat 2 minutes at highest speed. Pour into pan. Bake 25-35 minutes or till toothpick inserted comes out clean. Cool completely. Combine frosting and cream cheese at low speed till smooth. Frost. Store in refrigerator.

Frosted Spicy Pumpkin Bars

2 cups sifted flour
4 tsp. baking powder
1 1/4 tsp. cinnamon
1 tsp. nutmeg
1 tsp. ginger
1/2 tsp. salt
1/2 cup shortening

1 cup brown sugar,
  packed
1/4 cup sugar
4 eggs
1 (16 oz.) can pumpkin
  (2 cups)

Sift together flour, baking powder spices and salt; set aside. Cream together shortening, brown sugar and sugar in bowl until light and fluffy, using electric mixer at medium speed. Add eggs, one at a time, beating after each addition. Beat in pumpkin. Gradually stir dry ingredients into creamed mixture, mixing well. Spread mixture into greased 15 1/2 x 10 1/2 x 1 inch jelly roll pan. Bake in 350° oven 30 minutes or till top springs back when touched lightly with finger. Cool in pan or rack. Prepare and frost with Cream Cheese Icing.

Cream Cheese Frosting

Combine in bowl:

1 (3 oz.) pkg. softened
  cream cheese
1 tsp. grated lemon rind
pinch salt

1 Tbsp. margarine
2 1/2 cups sifted
  confectioners sugar
1 Tbsp. milk

Stir till smooth with spoon. May sprinkle chopped walnuts on top of bars if you wish.

Cream Cheese Pumpkin Bars

1 (16 oz.) pkg. golden
  pound cake mix
2 eggs
2 egg whites
2 Tbsp. margarine,
  melted
3/4 cup chopped nuts

3 tsp. pumpkin pie spice
1 (14 oz.) can sweetened
  condensed milk
1 (16 oz.) can pumpkin
1/2 tsp. salt
1 (8 oz.) pkg. cream
  cheese, softened

Preheat oven to 350°. In large bowl, combine cake mix, 1 egg, margarine, 1/2 cup nuts and 1 1/2 teaspoon pumpkin pie spice until crumbly. Press onto bottom of a 15 x 10 inch jelly roll pan; set aside. In large mixer bowl, beat cheese till fluffy. Gradually beat in sweetened condensed milk, then remaining egg and egg whites, pumpkin, remaining 1 1/2 teaspoon pumpkin pie spice and salt; mix well. Pour over crust; sprinkle 1/4 cup nuts on top. Bake 30 to 35 minutes or till set. Cool. Chill; cut into bars. Store in refrigerator.

Pumpkin Pie Bars

Crumb Crust:

1 1/2 cups rolled oats
1 1/2 cups flour
3/4 cup brown sugar
1/2 tsp. soda

3/4 cup margarine,
  melted
1/2 tsp. salt

Combine above. Pat 1/2 of mixture in greased 9 x 13 inch pan. Bake 8-10 minutes at 375°.

Filling:

2 cups pumpkin
2/3 cup milk
1 tsp. pumpkin pie spice

1/3 cup brown sugar
1 egg

Blend well. Pour into crust. Top with remaining crust. Bake 25 minutes. Cool. Cut. Refrigerate. Can be frozen.

Pumpkin Bars

(Microwave)

1 cup flour
3/4 cup brown sugar
1 cup pumpkin
1/2 tsp. baking powder
1/2 tsp. baking soda

1/4 tsp. salt
1 tsp. pumpkin pie spice
1/3 cup chopped nuts
1/4 cup raisins
1 egg

Place all ingredients in bowl. Blend at low speed; then beat at medium speed 1 minute. Spread batter in 8 x 8 inch baking dish. Place dish on inverted saucer. Microwave at 50% (medium) for 6 minutes rotating 1/4 turn every 1 to 2 minutes. Increase power to high. Microwave 5 to 6 minutes rotating 1/4 turn every 2 minutes, until very little unbaked batter appears through bottom of dish. Let stand 5 to 10 minutes. Cool before frosting.

Cream Cheese Frosting

1 (3 oz.) pkg. cream
    cheese
2 Tbsp. margarine

1 1/2 to 2 cups
    confectioners sugar

Combine cream cheese and margarine in mixing bowl. Microwave at high for 10 to 20 seconds or till softened. Blend well. Beat in sugar till of spreading consistency. Spread on cooled cake. Frosts 8 x 8 inch cake.

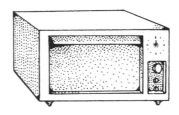

Streusel Pumpkin Pie Squares

1 cup sifted flour
1/2 cup quick-cooking
  oats
1/2 cup brown sugar
1/2 cup margarine
1 (16 oz.) pumpkin
1 (13 1/2 oz.) can
  evaporated milk
2 eggs

3/4 cup sugar
1 tsp. cinnamon
1/2 tsp. ginger
1/4 tsp. cloves
1/2 cup brown sugar,
  packed
1/2 tsp. salt
1/2 cup chopped pecans
2 Tbsp. margarine

Combine flour, oats, 1/2 cup brown sugar and 1/2 cup margarine in bowl. Mix till crumbly, using electric mixer at low speed. Press dough into bottom and 1/2 inch up sides of ungreased 13 x 9 x 2 inch baking pan. Bake at 350° for 15 minutes. Combine pumpkin, milk, eggs, sugar, spices and salt in bowl. Beat well using rotary beater. Pour into baked crust. Bake in 350° oven for 20 minutes. Combine pecans, 1/2 cup brown sugar and 2 tablespoons margarine; sprinkle over pumpkin filling. Return to oven and bake 15 minutes or till filling is set. Cool in pan on rack. Cut into 2 1/4 inch squares. Makes 24.

The Big Max variety of pumpkin can reach 70 inches in circumference, and is prized for carving into jack-o'-lanterns.

Pumpkin Cheesecake Bars

1 (16 oz. pkg.) pound
   cake mix
3 eggs
2 Tbsp. margarine or
   butter, melted
4 tsp. pumpkin pie spice
1 (8 oz.) pkg. cream
   cheese, softened

1 (14 oz.) can sweetened
   condensed milk
1 (16 oz.) can pumpkin
   (2 cups)
1/2 tsp. salt
1 cup chopped nuts

Preheat oven to 350°. In large mixer bowl on low speed, combine cake mix, 1 egg, margarine and 2 teaspoons pumpkin pie spice until crumbly. Press onto bottom of 15 x 10 inch jelly roll pan; set aside. In large mixer bowl, beat cream cheese until fluffy. Gradually beat in sweetened condensed milk, then remaining 2 eggs, pumpkin, remaining 2 teaspoons pumpkin pie spice and salt; mix well. Pour over crust, sprinkle nuts on top. Bake 30 or 35 minutes or until set. Cool. Cut into bars.

Pumpkin Cheesecake Bars

1 cup flour
1/3 cup firmly packed
  golden brown sugar
5 Tbsp. butter
1/2 cup finely chopped
  pecans or walnuts
1 pkg. (8 oz.) softened
  cream cheese

3/4 cup sugar
1/2 cup pumpkin
2 eggs
1 1/2 tsp. cinnamon
1 tsp. allspice
1 tsp. vanilla

Combine flour and brown sugar in medium bowl. Cut in butter to make a crumb mixture. Stir in nuts. Set aside 3/4 cup mixture for topping. Press remaining mixture into bottom of 8 x 8 x 1 1/2 inch baking pan. Bake at 350° for 15 minutes. Cool slightly. Combine cream cheese, sugar, pumpkin, eggs, spices and vanilla in large mixer bowl. Blend till smooth. Pour over baked crust. Sprinkle with reserved topping. Bake an additional 30 to 35 minutes. Cool before cutting into bars. Makes 32 (1 to 2 inch) bars.

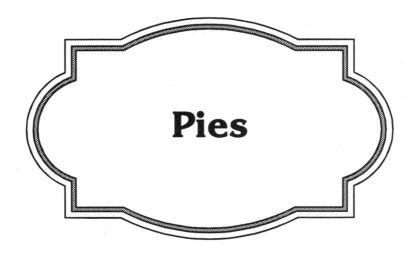

Pies

Foolproof Pie Crust

2 cups unbleached flour
1 tsp. salt
2/3 cup plus 2 Tbsp.
  melted margarine

1 Tbsp. cider vinegar
1/3 cup cold water

Mix dry ingredients, cut in melted margarine. Mix vinegar and cold water, add to flour mixture tossing and stirring as you add. Stir vigorously with fork until mixture holds together well, then form into ball. Roll out between wax paper sheets, as needed.

Easy Pumpkin Pie

1 cup pumpkin
1 scant cup sugar
2 eggs
1 heaping Tbsp.
  cinnamon

1 1/2 cups thick cream
1/2 cup milk
1/4 tsp. salt
1/4 tsp. cloves
1 unbaked pie shell

Mix. Pour into unbaked crust. Bake 10 minutes at 450°, then turn oven to 350°. Bake till knife inserted in center comes out clean. Cool.

Simple Pumpkin Pie

2 eggs
1 cup pumpkin
1 cup evaporated milk
pinch salt

1 scant cup sugar
1 tsp. cinnamon
1/2 tsp. nutmeg

Beat eggs, add to pumpkin. Add other ingredients gradually. Stir well. Bake at 425° for 10 minutes, then 375° for 20 minutes.

Old Fashioned Pumpkin Pie

1 egg
1 cup pumpkin
1/2 cup sugar
1 large Tbsp. flour

1 tsp. allspice
1 tsp. cinnamon
1 cup milk

Beat egg. Add to pumpkin. Add all ingredients. Mix well. Bake at 450° for 10 minutes. 350° until done.

Pumpkin Eggnog Pie

1 (9 inch) unbaked pie
  shell
1 (16 oz.) can pumpkin
  (2 cup)
1 1/2 cups eggnog
2 eggs

1/4 tsp. ginger
1/2 cup sugar
1/2 tsp. cinnamon
1/2 tsp. salt
1/4 tsp. cloves

Preheat oven to 425°. In large mixer bowl, combine all ingredients except pastry shell, mix well. Pour into pastry shell. Bake 15 minutes. Reduce to 350°, bake 40 to 45 minutes longer or till knife inserted near edge comes out clean. Refrigerate leftovers.

Pumpkin Pie

1/8 tsp. salt
2 tsp. pumpkin spice
2/3 cup sugar
2 eggs, slightly beaten

1 2/3 cups milk
1 1/2 cups mashed,
cooked pumpkin
1/2 recipe plain pastry

Sift dry ingredients together and stir into eggs. Add milk and pumpkin. Line pie pan with pastry and pour in filling. Bake in very hot oven (450° F.) 10 minutes. Reduce temperature to slow (325° F.) and bake 35 minutes longer or until knife inserted in center comes out clean. Cool. Makes 1 (9 inch) pie.

Pumpkin Nut:

Add 1/3 cup chopped nut meats to custard before baking. Use 1 teaspoon cinnamon, 1/4 teaspoon nutmeg and 1/2 teaspoon ginger instead of pumpkin pie spice.

Pumpkin Cream:

Mix 3/4 cup sugar, 2 tablespoons cornstarch and 2 teaspoons pumpkin pie spice. Add 1 egg yolk, 1 cup pumpkin and 2 cups milk. Cook until thickened, stirring constantly. Pour into baked pastry shell. Cover with meringue and bake.

Pumpkin Banana Pie

8 oz. pumpkin
4 eggs
1 banana, sliced
1 tsp. cinnamon
1/2 cup water

1/3 cup dry milk
1 Tbsp. brown sugar
replacement
1/2 tsp. nutmeg

Combine in blender. Pour into 2 (9 inch) shells. Bake at 350° for 45 minutes.

Pumpkin-Mallow Pie

1 cup cooked pumpkin
1 lb. marshmallows, cut
  in pieces
1/4 tsp. allspice
1/2 tsp. nutmeg
1 1/4 cups whipping
  cream
1 pastry shell

Combine all except cream in pan, heat and stir until marshmallows are completely melted, chill thoroughly. Beat mixture well with large spoon, gradually add whipped cream and beat until thoroughly mixed and smooth. Pour in baked pastry shell and chill until set.

Pumpkin seed tea is said to be good for the bladder and for killing tapeworm.

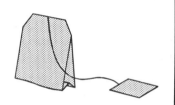

Mallow Pumpkin Pie

1 egg yolk, slightly beaten
3 egg yolks
1 1/2 cups pumpkin
2/3 cup sugar
1/2 tsp. ginger
1/4 tsp. nutmeg
1 ready-crust graham
  cracker pie crust
1/2 tsp. salt
1 1/4 tsp. cinnamon
1/4 tsp. cloves
1 1/2 cups evaporated milk

Brush egg yolk evenly on bottom and sides of crust, bake at 375° on baking sheet till light brown, about 5 minutes. Remove from oven. Combine 3 egg yolks, pumpkin, sugar, salt and spices. Gradually add evaporated milk; mix well. Pour into crust, bake at 375° on baking sheet 10 minutes or till knife inserted near center comes out clean. Cool before serving.

Pumpkin-Mince Pie

pastry for 9 inch pie shell
2 cups mincemeat
1/3 cup brown sugar
1/2 tsp. salt
1 tsp. cinnamon
1/4 tsp. ginger

1/4 tsp. cloves
1 cup canned pumpkin
2 eggs
3/4 cup evaporated milk
or cream

Line a 9 inch pie plate with pastry. Crimp edges. Spread the mincemeat over the bottom. Bake in hot oven 425° for 15 minutes. While this bakes, mix together brown sugar, salt and spices. Mix spice mixture with pumpkin. Beat eggs slightly and add milk. Stir into pumpkin mixture and mix thoroughly. Pour over mincemeat. Bake at 350° until custard is set, about 35 minutes.

Pumpkin-Mincemeat Pie

1 (9 or 10 inch)
  unbaked pastry shell
1 (9 oz.) pkg. condensed
  mincemeat, crumbled
3/4 cup water
1 (16 oz.) can pumpkin
2 eggs

1/2 tsp. salt
1 tsp. cinnamon
1/2 tsp. ginger
1/2 tsp. nutmeg
1 (14 oz.) sweetened
  condensed milk

Place rack in lowest position in oven, preheat oven to 425°. In small pan, combine mincemeat and water, bring to a boil. Cook and stir 1 minute. Turn into pastry shell. In large mixer bowl, combine remaining ingredients, mix well. Pour over mincemeat. Bake 15 minutes. Reduce temperature to 350°, bake 35 to 40 minutes longer or till set in center. Cool. Serve warm or chilled. Refrigerate leftovers.

Magic Pumpkin Pie

1 unbaked pie shell	1 egg
2 cups pumpkin	1/2 tsp. nutmeg
1 (15 oz.) can sweetened	1/2 tsp. ginger
condensed milk, *not*	3/4 tsp. cinnamon
evaporated	

Blend together and pour into pie shell. Bake at 375° for 50 minutes. Cool. Refrigerate at least 1 hour.

One of the best varieties of pumpkin for pies is the Small Sugar.

Honey Pumpkin Pie

1 1/2 cup pumpkin	1 tsp. vanilla
3/4 cup honey	4 beaten eggs
pinch baking soda	1 1/2 cups evaporated
1/2 tsp. salt	milk
1 tsp. cinnamon	1/4 cup melted butter
1/2 tsp. ginger	1 (10 inch) pie shell,
1/4 tsp. nutmeg	unbaked
1/2 tsp. cloves	

Mix pumpkin, honey and seasonings; beat well. Add eggs, milk and butter and beat till thoroughly mixed. Pour into unbaked pie shell and bake at 375° for 1 hour or till knife in center comes out clean. Note: the honey produces a shiny appearance on top of pie, as opposed to matte finish of pie with refined sugar. Be careful not to overbake because it doesn't look done.

Pumpkin Pie (Best Ever)

Prepare pastry and make an unbaked 9 inch pastry shell. Chill thoroughly. Blend together 3/4 cup sugar, 1/2 teaspoon salt to 2-3 teaspoons pumpkin spice. Beat 3 eggs, add 2 cups canned pumpkin. Add spices and sugar to the egg-pumpkin mixture, mix well. Add 2 cups milk gradually. Pour into unbaked pie shell, bake in preheated oven 450° for 10 minutes. Continue baking 350° for 40 minutes or until done.

> *Morton, Illinois is the pumpkin capital of the world.*

Spicy Rich Pumpkin Pie

pastry for 10 inch pie shell
3 cups canned pumpkin
1 cup sugar
1 cup brown sugar
1 tsp. nutmeg
1 tsp. cinnamon
1 tsp. ginger
1/4 tsp. cloves
1/4 tsp. allspice
1 tsp. salt
4 eggs
1/4 cup butter
whipped cream
maple sugar or syrup, optional
cheese, optional

Mix together pumpkin, sugars and spices. Add slightly beaten eggs with melted butter. Add to the pumpkin mixture and mix well. Pour into pastry shell. Bake in very hot oven, 450°, for 10 minutes. Reduce heat to 350° and bake 40 minutes longer, until the center is set. Cool. This pie is good frosted with whipped cream sweetened with maple sugar or syrup and served with cheese.

Pumpkin Pie (10-pie recipe)

5 cups sugar
5 tsp. ginger
6 Tbsp. cinnamon
2 tsp. cloves
1/4 cup orange juice
salt

1/2 cup cornstarch
1 (No. 10) can pumpkin
    (approximately 16 cups)
20 eggs, well beaten
1/2 cup molasses
4 qts. milk, scalded

Combine ingredients, adding salt to taste. Mix thoroughly. Pour into pastry lined pans. (Allow 3 1/2 cups of mixture per pie.) Bake in hot oven (425° F.) until a knife inserted in center comes out clean. 60 servings–1/6 pie per serving. Makes 10 pies (10 3/4 inches in diameter).

Frozen Pumpkin Pie

1 cup confectioners
    sugar
1 tsp. cinnamon
1 tsp. ginger
1/8 tsp. salt
3 eggs, separated

1 1/2 cups mashed
    cooked pumpkin
2/3 cup heavy cream,
    whipped
1 cookie pie shell

Add sugar, spices, salt and slightly beaten egg yolks to pumpkin and cook over boiling water till thickened. Fold in stiffly beaten egg whites, then cream. Pour into refrigerator tray and partially freeze. Pack into pie shell. Serve at once. 9 inch pie.

Cookie Pie Shell

1 1/2 cups fine crumbs,
    gingersnaps

1/4 cup sugar
1/2 cup butter, melted

Mix crumbs and sugar together; stir in butter. Line pan with mixture by pressing firmly into place. Chill 20 minutes or bake in moderate oven (350°) 10 minutes. Cool. Makes 1 (9 inch) pie shell.

Crustless Pumpkin Pie

1 Tbsp. unflavored gelatin
1/4 cup cold water
3 eggs, separated
2/3 cup honey
1 1/2 cups pumpkin

1/2 cup milk
1/2 tsp. salt
1 tsp. cinnamon
1/4 tsp. nutmeg
2 Tbsp. honey

Soak gelatin in water to soften. Beat yolks of eggs and combine with honey, pumpkin, milk, salt, cinnamon and nutmeg. Cook in top of double boiler, stirring constantly until mixture thickens. Remove from heat and add gelatin. Beat egg whites until frothy; dribble in honey and continue beating till stiff. Fold into pumpkin mixture. Pour into oiled 9 inch pie pan and chill several hours.

Traditional Pumpkin Pie

1 (9 inch) unbaked pie
    shell
1 (16 oz.) can pumpkin
1 (14 oz.) can sweetened
    condensed milk, not
    evaporated

1 tsp. cinnamon
1/2 tsp. ginger
1/2 tsp. nutmeg
1/2 tsp. salt
2 eggs

Preheat oven to 425°. In large bowl, combine all ingredients except pastry shell; mix well. Pour into pastry shell. Bake 15 minutes. Reduce heat to 350°, bake 35 to 40 minutes longer or till knife inserted comes out clean. Cook. Garnish as desired. Refrigerate leftovers. 9 inch pie.

Frost on the Pumpkin Pie

1 1/2 cups gingersnap
   cookie crumbs
1/4 cup margarine,
   melted
1 cup canned pumpkin

2 tsp. pumpkin pie spice
1/4 cup packed brown
   sugar
1 qt. butter pecan ice
   cream, softened

Mix together gingersnap crumbs and melted margarine. Press firmly against bottom and sides of 9 inch pie pan. Bake at 350° for 5 to 7 minutes. Cool. In small pan, combine pumpkin, sugar and pumpkin pie spice. Cook slowly until mixture is heated through; cool. Fold pumpkin mixture into softened ice cream. Pour into cooled gingersnap crust. Freeze pie 4 to 6 hours or overnight. Garnish with whipped cream.

Native American Indians of the eastern United States considered pumpkins nearly as important a food as corn and beans. They ate them baked, boiled and in soups and stews. Even the seeds were toasted or ground into meal for gruel or bread.

Frost on the Pumpkin Pie

Crust:

1 1/4 cup (18 squares)
 graham cracker
 crumbs
3 Tbsp. sugar
1/2 tsp. cinnamon

1/4 tsp. nutmeg
1/8 tsp. cloves
1/3 cup margarine,
 melted

Filling:

1 can Pillsbury ready to
 spread sour cream
 vanilla or vanilla
 frosting supreme
1 cup dairy sour cream
1 cup canned pumpkin

1/2 tsp. ginger
1/4 tsp. cloves
1 tsp. cinnamon
8 oz. carton (3 1/2 cup)
 frozen whipped
 topping, thawed

Heat oven to 350°. In small bowl, combine all crust ingredients, stir till blended. Reserve 2 tablespoons crumbs for topping. Press remaining crumbs over bottom and up sides of 9 or 10 inch pie pan. Bake at 350° for 6 minutes. Cool.

In large bowl, combine all filling ingredients except whipped topping; beat 2 minutes at medium speed. Fold in 1 cup whipped topping, pour into crust. Spread remaining whipped topping over filling. Sprinkle with reserved 2 tablespoons crumbs. Refrigerate at least 4 hours.

In ancient times, jack-o'-lanterns were carried to ward off evil spirits.

Deep-Dish Pumpkin Pie

1 3/4 cups unsifted flour
1/3 cup firmly packed
   brown sugar
1/3 cup sugar
1 cup cold margarine,
   cut into small pieces
1 cup chopped nuts

1 (16 oz.) can pumpkin
   (2 cup)
1 (14 oz.) can sweetened
   condensed milk
2 eggs
1 tsp. cinnamon
1/2 tsp. allspice
1/2 tsp. salt

Preheat oven to 350°. In medium bowl, combine flour and sugars; cut in margarine till crumbly. Stir in nuts. Reserving 1 cup crumb mixture, press remainder firmly on bottom and halfway up sides of 12 x 7 inch baking dish. In large mixer bowl, combine remaining ingredients except reserved crumb mixture. Mix well. Pour into prepared dish. Top with reserved crumb mixture. Bake 55 minutes or till golden. Cool. Serve with ice cream if desired. Refrigerate leftovers.

What did the pumpkin sew?
A pumpkin patch.

Deep Dish Pumpkin Pie (custard)

Put 2 cups mashed pumpkin into a basin, add 1 cup sugar, 4 beaten egg yolks, 4 cups milk, 1/2 teaspoon cinnamon, 1/4 teaspoon mace, 1/4 teaspoon grated nutmeg and 4 egg whites, beaten stiff. Line a very deep pie dish with some good pastry. Pour in pumpkin custard. Bake at approximately 350° till done.

Orange Pumpkin Pie

2 Tbsp. unflavored gelatin
1/4 cup cold water
2 1/2 cups pumpkin
1 1/4 cup brown sugar
1/2 tsp. salt
1 1/2 tsp. pumpkin pie
  spice
1/3 cup orange juice
2 cups milk
2 egg yolks, slightly
  beaten
2 Tbsp. butter
1 baked pie shell

Soften gelatin in water 5 minutes. Combine next 8 ingredients in order listed and cook in top of double boiler till slightly thickened. Add gelatin and stir till dissolved. Cool. Pour into pastry shell and chill until firm. Makes 10 inch pie.

Dietetic Orange Pumpkin Pie

1 (8 inch) pie crust
1 cup canned pumpkin
2 eggs
3/4 cup skim milk
1/4 tsp. salt
6 oz. can frozen orange
  juice concentrate,
  defrosted and undiluted
1/2 Tbsp. cornstarch
2 tsp. pumpkin pie spice

Combine ingredients in bowl and beat them thoroughly. Pour mixture into prepared pastry shell. Bake for 1 hour in preheated 350° oven.

Pie Crust

1/2 cup flour
2 Tbsp. salad oil
pinch salt
1 Tbsp. ice water

Stir all together, knead lightly until forms ball. Flatten out dough, wrap in wax paper and chill thoroughly. Roll out on lightly floured board; fit into pie dish.

Praline Pumpkin Pie

1 (9 inch) pie shell
1 Tbsp. margarine
1 cup chopped pecans
1/4 cup margarine
1/3 cup packed brown
  sugar
1/3 cup sugar

1 (2 1/4 or 3 oz.) pkg.
  no-bake custard mix
2 tsp. pumpkin pie spice
1 (16 oz.) can (2 cup)
  pumpkin
2/3 cup milk
1 (5 1/3 oz.) can (2/3
  cup) evaporated milk

Prepare pastry, bake 450° for 10 to 12 minutes or till golden. Cool thoroughly on rack.

To toast pecans, dot 1 tablespoon margarine over pecans in a shallow baking pan. Bake in 350° oven for 15 minutes or till toasted, stirring often. For filling: in a small pan melt the 1/4 cup margarine. Stir in brown sugar and 1/2 cup toasted pecans; cook and stir till bubbly. Spread over bottom of baked pastry shell; cool to room temperature. In medium pan, combine sugar, custard mix, and pumpkin pie spice. Stir in pumpkin, milk and evaporated milk. Cook and stir till bubbly. Cover and cool 10 minutes. Carefully pour pumpkin mixture over pecans in pastry shell. Chill pie till firm before serving. Garnish top with additional toasted pecans. Cover and chill to store.

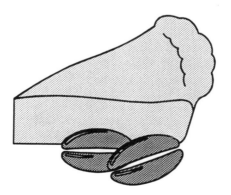

Pecan Pumpkin Pie

3 eggs
1 cup pumpkin
1/3 cup sugar
1 tsp. pumpkin pie spice
2/3 cup corn syrup

1/2 cup sugar
3 Tbsp. melted butter
1/2 tsp. vanilla
1 cup pecan halves

Stir together 1 slightly beaten egg, pumpkin, 1/3 cup sugar and pie spice. Spread over bottom of pie shell. Combine 2 beaten eggs, corn syrup, 1/2 cup sugar, butter and vanilla. Stir in nuts. Spoon over pumpkin mixture. Bake in 350° F. oven for 50 minutes or until filling is set. Put filling into 9 inch pie crust.

Pumpkin-Pecan Pie

4 eggs, slightly beaten
2 cups pumpkin
1 cup sugar
1/2 cup dark corn syrup
1 tsp. vanilla
1/2 tsp. cinnamon

1/4 tsp. salt
1 cup chopped pecans
1 unbaked 9 inch pastry
   shell
orange rind strips
pecan halves

Combine eggs, pumpkin, sugar, syrup, vanilla, cinnamon and salt in a medium bowl; stir until well blended. Pour into pastry shell; sprinkle with pecans. Bake at 350° for 1 hour and 10 minutes or till pie is firm in center. Let cool completely. Before serving, garnish with orange rind strips and pecan halves.

Delicious Pumpkin-Pecan Pie

4 lbs. fresh pumpkin (3
  3/4 cup)
1 (14 oz.) can sweetened
  condensed milk
2 eggs
1 tsp. cinnamon
1/2 tsp. nutmeg

1/2 tsp. ginger
1/2 tsp. salt
pastry for 9 inch pie
1/2 cup pecan halves
3 Tbsp. dark brown sugar
3 Tbsp. whipping cream

Combine 3 3/4 cup pumpkin, milk, eggs and seasonings in processor bowl. Pulse just until blended. Fit pastry into pie plate, pour pumpkin mixture into pastry shell. Bake at 375° for 50-55 minutes or till knife inserted halfway between center and edge of pie comes out clean. Cool slightly. Sprinkle chopped pecans around outer edge of pie. Combine sugar and whipping cream in small pan; cook over medium heat, stirring constantly, until sugar dissolves. Reduce heat and simmer 5 minutes; let cool 5 minutes. Spoon over pecans.

Note: 2 cans pumpkin may be substituted for 3 3/4 cup fresh pumpkin.

*For large pumpkins, sow
seed on hills made over the spent
manure from a mushroom bed
or a hotbed.*

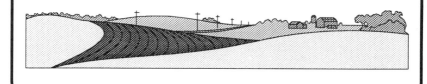

Mary's Pumpkin Meringue Pie

1 (9 inch) baked pastry
   shell
3/4 cup sugar
3 Tbsp. cornstarch
1/2 tsp. salt
1/2 tsp. cinnamon
1/2 tsp. ginger

1/4 tsp. nutmeg
1/8 tsp. cloves
2 cups milk
1 cup canned pumpkin
3 eggs
meringue for pie

In pan, combine sugar, cornstarch, salt and spices. Gradually stir in milk and pumpkin. Cook and stir till thickened and bubbly. Reduce heat; cook and stir 2 minutes more. Remove from heat. Separate egg yolk from whites; set whites aside for meringue. Beat egg yolks slightly. Gradually stir 1 cup of the hot mixture into yolks. Return mixture to pan, bring to gentle boil. Cook and stir 2 minutes more. Pour hot mixture into baked pastry shell. Make meringue for pie. Spread meringue over the hot filling; seal to edge. Bake in 350° oven for 12 to 15 minutes or till golden. Cool. Cover. Chill to store.

Meringue:

3 egg whites
1/4 tsp. cream of tartar

1/2 tsp. vanilla
6 Tbsp. sugar

Beat egg whites, vanilla and cream of tartar for 1 minute. Gradually add sugar, 1 tablespoon at a time beating at high speed, till glossy and sugar dissolves, about 4 minutes.

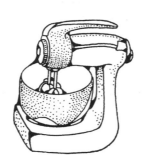

Pumpkin Meringue Pie

1/8 tsp. salt	2 eggs, slightly beaten
2/3 cup sugar	1 2/3 cups milk
2 tsp. pumpkin pie spice	1 1/2 cups cooked
1 pie shell	pumpkin

Stir dry ingredients together and stir into eggs. Add milk and pumpkin. Pour into pie shell. Bake very hot (450°) 10 minutes. Reduce (325°) and bake 35 minutes longer. Cool.

Pumpkin-Nut: add 1/3 cup chopped nut meats to custard before baking.

Pumpkin Cream: mix 3/4 cup sugar, 2 tablespoons cornstarch and 2 teaspoons pumpkin pie spice. Add 1 egg yolk, 1 cup pumpkin and 2 cups milk. Cook till thickened, stirring constantly, pour into baked pie shell, cover with meringue and bake.

Can use 1 teaspoon cinnamon, 1/4 teaspoon nutmeg and 1/2 teaspoon ginger instead of pumpkin pie spice.

Pumpkins grow on both vines and bushes, although those that grow on bushes are much smaller than those that grow on sprawling vines.

Basic Pumpkin Pie

1 (16 oz.) can pumpkin
3/4 cup sugar
1 tsp. cinnamon
1/2 tsp. salt
1/2 tsp. ginger
1/2 tsp. nutmeg
3 eggs
1 (5 1/3 oz.) can (2/3 cup) evaporated milk
1/2 cup milk
unsweetened whipped cream, optional
1 (9 inch) unbaked pie shell

Combine pumpkin, sugar, cinnamon, salt, ginger and nutmeg. Add eggs, lightly beat egg in with a fork, add evaporated milk and milk, mix well. Bake 375° for 25 minutes with foil over edge of pie, remove foil and bake 25 to 30 minutes longer. Garnish with whipped cream.

Honey Pumpkin Pie: omit the 3/4 cup sugar and add 1/2 cup honey to pumpkin mixture.

Raisin-Pumpkin Pie: add 1/8 teaspoon cloves and 3/4 cup light raisins to pumpkin mixture.

Molasses-Pumpkin Pie: decrease sugar to 1/2 cup and add 1/3 cup molasses to pumpkin mixture.

Caramel Pumpkin Pie

2 1/2 cups pumpkin
1/4 cup cream
2 eggs, slightly beaten
1 cup sugar
1 Tbsp. flour
1 tsp. pumpkin pie spice

1/4 tsp. lemon extract
1/2 tsp. vanilla
1 Tbsp. melted butter
1 (9 inch) pie shell,
   uncooked

Mix pumpkin, cream and eggs. Add sugar, flour and spice. Mix well. Add butter and flavorings. Mix and pour into pie shell. Bake in hot oven, 425°, for 10 minutes. Reduce heat to 375° and bake until knife inserted into center comes out clean (about 1 1/2 hours). Top with the following mixture.

Topping:

1 cup pecan meats
1/4 cup melted butter

1 cup brown sugar

Serve with whipped cream.

Pumpkin Pie Filling
(Sugarless)

3/4 cup nonfat dry milk
   solids
1/2 tsp. salt
1/2 tsp. cinnamon
2 eggs
1/2 tsp. mace
2 Tbsp. melted margarine

1/4 tsp. cloves
1 1/2 cups pumpkin
1/2 tsp. ginger
3/4 cup strained honey
1 1/2 cups water
1 (9 inch) unbaked
   pastry shell

Mix dry ingredients well to prevent streaking. Add other ingredients. Blend thoroughly. Turn into pastry shell. Bake 15 minutes at 425° in preheated oven. Reduce to 350° and bake 40 minutes longer.

Sour Cream-Pumpkin Pie

1 cup sugar
1/4 tsp. salt
1/2 tsp. ginger
1 tsp. cinnamon
1/4 tsp. nutmeg
1/4 tsp. cloves

1 (16 oz.) can pumpkin
1 (8 oz.) carton sour
  cream
3 eggs, separated
1 unbaked 9 inch pie
  shell

Combine first 6 ingredients; add pumpkin and sour cream, stirring well. Beat egg yolks until thick and lemon colored; stir into pumpkin mixture. Beat egg whites (at room temperature) until stiff peaks form; fold into pumpkin mixture. Pour into pastry shell. Bake at 450° for 10 minutes; reduce heat to 350° and bake 55 minutes or until set.

Pumpkin Creme Pie

2 cups gingersnap
  cookie crumbs
1/3 cup margarine, melted
1 1/2 cups canned
  pumpkin pie mix
1 (7 oz.) jar
  marshmallow creme

2 (8 oz.) containers (3
  cup each) whipped
  topping with real
  cream, thawed
pecan halves
1 tsp. rum flavoring, op-
  tional

Combine crumbs and margarine. Reserve 1/4 cup crumb mixture; press remaining mixture onto bottom and sides of 9 inch pie plate. Chill. Combine pie mix, marshmallow creme and flavoring, mixing with electric mixer or wire whisk until well blended. Fold in one container of whipped topping; pour into crust. Sprinkle with reserved crumbs. Cover; freeze. Place in refrigerator 30 minutes before serving. Top with remaining whipped topping and pecans.

Pumpkin Pie Topping

2/3 cup coarsely broken pecans

2/3 cup brown sugar
3 Tbsp. butter

Mix pecans with brown sugar and melted butter. Sprinkle the mixture over the top of your favorite pumpkin pie. Slide it under the broiler or place it in a hot oven, 425°, just until the top begins to melt.

Frosty Pumpkin Pie
(Microwave)

1/4 cup margarine
1 1/2 cups gingersnap crumbs
1/4 cup packed brown sugar
1/2 tsp. ginger
1/2 tsp. nutmeg
1/2 tsp. cinnamon

dash salt
1 cup canned pumpkin
1 pt. (2 cup) butter pecan ice cream
1/4 cup chopped pecans
1 carton (4 1/2 oz.) frozen whipped topping, defrosted

Place margarine in 9 inch pie plate. Microwave at high 1 to 1-1/2 minutes or till melted. Stir in crumbs till moistened. Press firmly and evenly against bottom and sides of pie plate. Microwave at high 1 to 1 1/2 minutes or till set, rotating 1/2 turn after 1 minute. Cool. In 3 quart bowl, mix sugar, spices and salt. Place ice cream in medium bowl. Reduce power to 50% (medium). Microwave 10 to 20 seconds or till softened; stir. Fold into pumpkin mixture. Add pecans. Fold in whipped topping. Pour into cooled pie shell. Freeze at least 6 hours or overnight.

Pumpkin Pie

(Microwave)

3 eggs, separated
1 cup canned pumpkin
1/2 cup packed brown
 sugar
1 1/3 cups evaporated
 milk

1 Tbsp. flour
1 tsp. cinnamon
1/4 tsp. salt
1/4 tsp. ginger
1/4 tsp. nutmeg

Blend 1 egg yolk in medium bowl or 2 quart casserole at low speed. Reserve the white. With soft brush, coat the shell (see below) with some beaten yolk to seal holes. Microwave at high 30 to 60 seconds or until yolk is set. Add 2 eggs and remaining ingredients, except the egg white, to leftover beaten yolk. Blend well at low speed. Beat white until soft mounds form. Stir into pumpkin mixture. Microwave at high 3 minutes stirring after 1 1/2 minutes. Reduce power to 50% (medium). Microwave 6 to 7 minutes or till mixture is very hot and slightly thickened stirring with wire whisk after 2 minutes, then every minute. Pour into shell. Fill to about 1/4 inch of top; flute. Set pie on wax paper in oven. Microwave at 50% (medium) 11 to 26 minutes or till set in center, rotating 1/4 turn every 4 minutes. Cool completely.

Microwave Crust:

1/3 cup shortening
2 Tbsp. margarine, room
 temperature
3 Tbsp. cold water

1 cup flour
1/2 tsp. salt
3 to 4 drops yellow food
 coloring, optional

Make as a regular crust. Shells must be microwaved before filling or the crust will not cook properly. Microwave at high 5 to 7 minutes rotating 1/2 turn every 3 minutes. Watch closely, crust will not brown but appear dry and opaque. 9 inch pie.

Pumpkin Chiffon Pie

3 egg yolks, beaten
3/4 cup packed brown
   sugar
1 1/2 cups cooked
   pumpkin
1/2 cup milk
1 baked pie shell

1 tsp. cinnamon
1/2 tsp. nutmeg
1 envelope (1 Tbsp.)
   unflavored gelatin
3 egg whites
1/4 cup sugar

Combine egg yolks, brown sugar, pumpkin, milk and spices in top of double boiler. Cook until it thickens, stirring constantly. Soften gelatin in 1/4 cup cold water. Stir into hot mixture, stirring until dissolved. Beat egg whites until soft peaks form. Add sugar gradually, beating until stiff. Fold into pumpkin mixture. Pour into pie shell. Chill until set. Serve with whipped cream.

Pumpkin Chiffon Pie

3 eggs, separated
1 cup sugar
1/2 tsp. mace
1 tsp. vanilla extract
2 envelopes unflavored
   gelatin
1/2 cup cold milk

1 cup milk, scalded
2 cups pumpkin
cookie crumbs (or
   graham cracker)
   for shell
ginger cookie crumbs,
   browned in butter

Beat egg yolks; add sugar, vanilla and mace. Mix well. Soften gelatin in cold milk. Add egg-sugar mixture, a little at a time, to the scalded milk, stirring constantly. Cook over low heat until thick. Stir in softened gelatin, blend and add pumpkin. Place in refrigerator until almost set. Beat egg whites stiff and fold into cold pumpkin mix. Turn into the crumb pie shell. Sprinkle with browned cookie crumbs. Refrigerate until set. Serves 6-8.

Layered Pumpkin Chiffon Pie

1 gingersnap-graham
  crust
1/3 cup sugar
1 envelope unflavored
  gelatin
1/2 tsp. salt
1/2 tsp. cinnamon
1/2 tsp. allspice
1/4 tsp. ginger
1/4 tsp. nutmeg

3 slightly beaten eggs
1 cup canned pumpkin
1/2 cup milk
3 egg whites
1/4 cup sugar
1 cup whipping cream
1/2 tsp. vanilla
1/4 tsp. cinnamon
1/4 cup powdered sugar

Prepare crust using 3/4 cup fine gingersnap crumbs (12 cookies), 1/2 cup fine graham cracker crumbs (7), 1/4 cup margarine, melted, and 2 tablespoons sugar. Press into pie plate, bake at 375° for 4 to 5 minutes. Cool. In pan, combine the 1/3 cup sugar, gelatin, salt, 1/2 teaspoon cinnamon, allspice, ginger and nutmeg. Combine egg yolks, pumpkin and milk; stir into gelatin mixture. Cook and stir over medium heat till gelatin dissolves and mixture thickens slightly. Remove from heat. Chill gelatin mixture to consistency of corn syrup, stirring occasionally. Immediately beat egg whites till soft peaks form. Gradually add 1/4 cup sugar, beating till stiff peaks form. When gelatin is consistency of unbeaten egg whites (partially set), fold in stiff-beaten egg whites. Pile *half* the egg white-gelatin mixture into baked crumb crust; set remainder aside. Combine whipping cream, powdered sugar, vanilla and 1/4 teaspoon cinnamon. Cover and refrigerate half the mixture. Whip remaining half till soft peaks form; spread over egg white-gelatin layer in crumb crust. Top with remaining gelatin mixture; chill several hours or overnight till set. To serve, whip reserved whipping cream mixture and pass with pie.

Pumpkin Chiffon Pie

1 envelope unflavored
gelatin
1/4 cup bourbon
3 eggs, separated
1 (16 oz.) can pumpkin
3/4 cup firmly packed
brown sugar
1/2 tsp. salt

2 tsp. pumpkin pie spice
1/2 cup milk
1/4 tsp. cream of tartar
1/4 cup plus 2 Tbsp.
sugar
1 unbaked 9 inch pastry
shell
Ginger Cream Topping

Soften gelatin in bourbon; let stand 5 minutes. Beat egg yolks slightly. Combine gelatin mixture, egg yolks, pumpkin, brown sugar, salt, pumpkin pie spice and milk in top of a double boiler. Cook over boiling water, stirring occasionally, about 10 minutes or till thoroughly heated. Chill until mixture mounds when dropped from a spoon. Beat egg whites (room temperature) and cream of tartar until foamy. Gradually add sugar, beating till stiff peaks form. Fold into pumpkin mixture; spoon into prepared pastry shell. Chill several hours until firm. To serve, top with Ginger Cream Topping.

Ginger Cream Topping:

1/2 tsp. ginger
1 cup whipping cream

1 Tbsp. sugar

Combine all ingredients; beat at medium-high speed of electric mixer until stiff peaks form.

Pumpkin Chiffon Pie

2 pkgs. French vanilla
   instant pudding
1 cup milk
1 (16 oz.) can pumpkin

1 tub Cool Whip (reg. size)
1 tsp. pumpkin pie spice
1 pastry shell

Mix until slightly thickened. Add 1 can pumpkin, 1/2 carton Cool Whip (regular size), teaspoon pumpkin pie spice. Pour into baked pie shell. Top with other half of Cool Whip and chill for several hours.

How To Carve a Jack-o'-Lantern

Cut out a section of pumpkin around the stem, keeping it in one piece. Lift out and save for the "lid." Use a large spoon to scoop everything out of the pumpkin. Scrape the walls free of excess membrane and seeds. (Save the seeds for roasting.) Carve out the eyes, nose and mouth, or use another food, such as a carrot, for the nose. Make "white" teeth or eyes by carving only the surface of the skin, then peeling it away. Make a hole in the center of the pumpkin floor. Insert a candle and light it. Replace the "lid" and enjoy the scary effect!

Pumpkin-Apple Pie

1 (9 inch) pastry shell
(baked 5 minutes at
450°); cooled
1/2 cup packed brown
sugar
1/2 cup water
2 Tbsp. margarine
1 Tbsp. cornstarch
1 tsp. cinnamon
1/2 tsp. salt
4 cups sliced, peeled,
cooking apples

1 Tbsp. lemon juice
1 slightly beaten egg
1 cup canned pumpkin
1/2 cup sugar
1/2 tsp. ginger
1/8 tsp. cloves
1 (5 1/3 oz.) can (2/3
cup) evaporated milk
unsweetened whipped
cream

In pan, combine brown sugar, water, margarine, corn-starch, cinnamon, and 1/4 teaspoon salt. Cook and stir over medium heat till mixture comes to boiling. Stir in sliced apples. Cover and cook for 5 to 6 minutes or till apples are crisp-tender, stirring occasionally. Remove from heat; stir in lemon juice. Spread apple mixture evenly in bottom of partially baked pastry shell. In mixing bowl, combine egg, pumpkin, sugar, ginger, cloves and remaining 1/4 teaspoon salt. Mix well. Stir in milk. Carefully pour pumpkin mixture over apples. To prevent overbrowning, cover edge of pie with foil. Bake in 375° oven for 20 minutes. Remove foil, bake for 20 to 25 minutes more or till knife inserted off-center comes out clean. Cool pie thoroughly. Serve with whipped cream. Cover, chill to store.

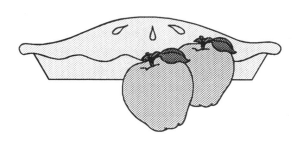

Almond Pumpkin Pie

1 (9 inch) unbaked pie shell
1 (16 oz.) can pumpkin (2 cup)
1 (14 oz.) can sweetened condensed milk
2 eggs
1 tsp. almond extract
1/2 tsp. cinnamon
1 (6 oz.) pkg. almond brickle chips or 1 cup almonds toasted and chopped finely

Preheat oven to 425°. In large mixer bowl, combine all ingredients except shell and brickle chips, mix well. Stir in 1/2 cup brickle chips. Pour into pastry shell. Top with remaining brickle chips. Bake 15 minutes. Reduce oven temperature to 350°. Bake 30 minutes longer or till knife inserted near center comes out clean. Cool. Refrigerate leftovers.

Early American cookbooks provided recipes for "pompkin" pudding that were more like pies. Baked in a crust, the filling ingredients were similar to those used today in a Thanksgiving Day pie.

One early American recipe for pumpkin pie called for layers of raw apple and raw pumpkin, sliced and heavily sugared, topped with a crust. This "pumpkin pie" was more like today's deep-dish apple pie.

Pumpkin Ice Cream Pie

1 pt. vanilla ice cream,
  softened
1 baked 9 inch pastry
  shell, chilled
1 cup canned pumpkin
3/4 cup sugar

1/2 tsp. ginger
1/2 tsp. cinnamon
1/4 tsp. nutmeg
1/2 tsp. salt
1 cup whipping cream,
  whipped

Spread ice cream evenly in chilled pastry shell; freeze. Combine next 6 ingredients, mixing well. Fold in whipped cream. Spread pumpkin mixture evenly over ice cream; freeze pie. Remove pie from freezer 15 minutes before serving.

Pumpkin Ice Cream Pie

(Microwave)

1 qt. vanilla ice cream
1 cup canned pumpkin
1/2 cup packed brown
  sugar

graham cracker crust
1 tsp. cinnamon
1/4 tsp. nutmeg
1/4 tsp. ginger

Graham Cracker Crust

5 Tbsp. margarine
2 Tbsp. white or brown
  sugar

1 1/3 cups fine graham
  cracker crumbs

Prepare crust: melt margarine in 9 inch pie plate at high 30 to 60 seconds. Stir in crumbs and sugar till well moistened. Press crumbs firmly and evenly against bottom and sides of plate. Microwave 1 1/2 minutes rotating 1/2 turn after 1 minute. Cool. Place ice cream in large bowl. Divide into fourths. Microwave at 50% (medium) 45 to 60 seconds or until lightly softened. Do not let ice cream melt. Mix in flavorings at lowest speed of electric mixture until well distributed. Spoon filling into pie shell. Freeze 2 hours or overnight until firm. If desired, top with chopped walnuts or pecans.

Pumpkin Ice Cream Pie

2 Zagnut® bars (1.75 oz. each), crushed
2/3 cup graham cracker crumbs
3 Tbsp. butter, melted
1 cup pumpkin
1/3 cup packed brown sugar, dark
1/2 tsp. cinnamon
1/4 tsp. nutmeg
1/8 tsp. cloves, ground
1 qt. vanilla ice cream, softened
1 cup whipping cream, whipped
1 Zagnut® bar (1.75 oz.), coarsely chopped

In bowl, combine first 3 ingredients; mix well. Press mixture firmly into bottom and along sides of 9 inch pie plate. Chill 1 hour. In large bowl, combine pumpkin, sugar and spices. Add softened ice cream; mix well. Pour into chilled crust. Freeze until firm. Remove from freezer 5 minutes before serving. Spread whipped cream over top. Sprinkle with chopped Zagnut bar.

Ice Cream Pumpkin Pie

2 pts. vanilla ice cream
2 Tbsp. chopped candied ginger
1 (9 inch) baked pie shell
1 cup canned pumpkin
1 cup sugar
1 tsp. pumpkin pie spice
1/2 tsp. ginger
1/2 tsp. salt
1/2 cup chopped walnuts
1 cup whipped cream

Stir ice cream to soften. Quickly fold in candied ginger and spread in pie shell. Freeze till ice cream is solid. Blend together pumpkin, sugar, spice, ginger, salt and nuts. Fold in whipped cream. Pour over frozen ice cream in pie shells. Freeze until firm. Shortly before serving, remove from freezer and put in refrigerator 10 minutes. Serves 8.

Rich Pumpkin Pie

3/4 cup sugar
2 Tbsp. cornstarch
1/2 tsp. cinnamon
1/2 tsp. mace
1/2 tsp. salt
1/4 tsp. ginger

1/4 tsp. allspice
1 cup pumpkin
1 1/4 cups evaporated milk
2 Tbsp. butter
3 eggs
1/4 tsp. vanilla

Mix sugar, cornstarch and spices, blend with pumpkin and milk mixture. Cook over boiling water 20 minutes. Beat eggs enough to make smooth. Add custard to eggs, cook again 2 minutes. Add vanilla. Cool and put in baked shell. Chill at least 6 hours. Serve with whipped cream or topping.

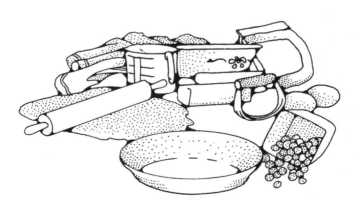

And More

Preparation of Pumpkin Meat

The secret of really good pumpkin recipes is in the preparation of the pumpkin. Cook very slowly until it has lost most of its moisture and has taken on a rich, golden brown color.

Pumpkin Puree

To make pumpkin puree for pie filling, cut a pumpkin in half crosswise and remove the seeds and stringy material. Cover the cut side of each pumpkin half with a piece of aluminum foil. Place the pumpkin halves on a baking sheet and bake, foil side up, in a preheated oven (350°) for about 1 1/2 hours or until the flesh is very tender when a fork is stuck into it. When the pumpkin is cool enough to handle, scoop out the flesh and mash it in a food processor, or force it through a sieve. If the puree is watery, drain it in a colander lined with cheesecloth. A 2 to 3 pound pumpkin yields about 2 to 3 cups puree.

Fried Pumpkin

In an iron skillet, generously greased with bacon drippings, place at least 2 cups cooked thinly sliced pumpkin with salt and pepper to taste and cook over high heat for 10 minutes, stirring occasionally. When it begins to brown, scrape from skillet into a platter and serve.

Fried Pumpkin

Using 6-8 inch young tender pumpkin, slice into 1/2 inch x 2 inch strips. Salt and pepper. Roll in flour and deep fry until brown on both sides.

Stewed Pumpkin

2 pts. cooked pumpkin	1 tsp. cinnamon
4 Tbsp. butter	1 tsp. cloves
1 tsp. salt	1 cup whiskey or brandy
1 tsp. mace	

Cut pumpkin into halves, then quarters and pare. Cut into pieces of about 1 inch square. Place in deep pot and add water to cover. Let the pumpkin stew slowly for about 1 hour, stirring frequently to prevent burning. Take out of pot, press through a colander and set back on stove. Add for every pint of pumpkin, 2 large tablespoonfuls of butter and 1/2 teaspoon of salt, 1 of mace, cinnamon and allspice. 1 cup of good whiskey or brandy may be added and improves the flavor. Mix all thoroughly and add sugar to taste. Let simmer for 1/2 hour longer and serve hot.

Baked Pumpkin

1 small pumpkin   **a dressing of butter or gravy**

Cut pumpkin in halves, then into quarters. 2 quarters are enough for a family of 6, if pumpkin is large. Remove seeds, but do not peel the rind. Place in baking pan with rind downwards and bake till tender (may be easily pierced with a fork). Serve in the rind at the table, scooping it out by spoonfuls. It is eaten with butter or gravy.

Dried Pumpkin

When they are full ripe, split them open, take out the seeds, cut the pumpkin up in long slices 1/2 inch thick, put them on a string and hang them in a dry place where air can have full admittance to them, which will dry them in a short time, but let them still hang through winter to secure them from all possibility of molding. Before you cook them, pour boiling water on and let them remain for a few hours to soften, then cut them in small pieces, parboil, and stew till very soft with a piece of tolerably fat pork; then mash fine and serve with the pork. This is a homely dish, but to most tastes–a very good one.

Freezing Pumpkin

Cut pumpkin in half. Take out seeds, turn upside down on cookie sheet, bake until soft. When tender, scoop out pumpkin and blend till smooth with as little water as possible. Freeze.

Note: see recipe for discarded seeds.

Pumpkin Soup

1 large onion, chopped
1/4 cup butter
1/2 tsp. curry powder
1 (16 oz.) can pumpkin
1 1/2 tsp. salt
2 cups half & half

2 1/2 cups chicken broth
chopped parsley, commercial sour cream or ground cinnamon, optional

Sauté onion in butter until tender; sprinkle with curry powder and sauté an additional 2 minutes. Stir in pumpkin and salt; add half & half, stirring constantly. Stir in broth and heat thoroughly. Garnish, if desired. For a richer soup, add more half & half to this recipe; for a thinner version, add more broth.

Pumpkin Soup

Melt in heavy kettle:

2 Tbsp. margarine

Add:

1/4 cup chopped green pepper

1 small onion, finely chopped

Sauté until soft but not brown. Blend in:

2 Tbsp. flour
1 tsp. salt

Add:

2 cups chicken broth or stock
2 cups milk
1/4 tsp. nutmeg

2 cups pumpkin
1/8 tsp. thyme
1 tsp. chopped parsley

Cook, stirring constantly, until slightly thickened.

Pumpkin Soup

1/2 cup chopped onion
1 Tbsp. minced parsley
4 Tbsp. butter
2 cans (1 lb. 13 oz. each)
  pumpkin
2 cans (No. 2) crushed
  pineapple

1 cup water
1/4 cup cornstarch
2 cups milk
2 cups light cream
1 tsp. salt

Sauté onions and parsley in butter. Add pumpkin and pineapple. Cook 10 minutes over low heat stirring frequently. Add water, cover and cook over low 30 minutes. Mix cornstarch with milk. Stir into pumpkin mixture, mixing steadily to boiling point. Blend in cream and salt. Cook over low 10 minutes. Serves 6-8.

Pumpkin Soup

1 (1 lb. 13 oz.) can
  pumpkin
1 clove garlic, crushed
1 Tbsp. Worcestershire
  sauce

6 cups broth
1/2 tsp. salt
1/4 tsp. pepper

Press pumpkin through a sieve. Add the garlic and Worcestershire sauce. Any kind of broth may be used–canned or water with bouillon powder or cubes or, best of all, broth made from a ham bone. Add the broth and stir well. Season to taste. Seasonings will depend entirely on the broth used. This may be served hot or cold. Yield: 2 quarts.

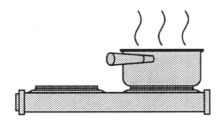

Pumpkin Soup

2 cups pumpkin, pared
    and diced
2 cups water
3 tsp. sugar

6 tsp. butter
1/2 tsp. salt
3 cups milk

Put pumpkin, water, half of butter, sugar and salt in a saucepan. Bring to a boil, cook 15 minutes or until pumpkin is soft. Rub through a sieve, add milk and bring back to a boil. Correct the seasoning and add remaining butter. Serve with tapioca that has been cooked in it or with crusts of bread on top. Serves 4-6.

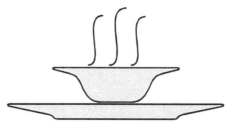

Chicken Pumpkin Soup

2 cups pumpkin
2 medium onions
1 Tbsp. unsalted butter
3 cups defatted chicken
    broth

dash nutmeg or allspice
freshly ground pepper,
    to taste
1 cup plain yogurt
chopped chives, for
    garnish

Steam pumpkin till tender, about 15-20 minutes, and set aside. In saucepan, sauté onions in butter over medium heat till translucent. Add pumpkin and cook for 5 minutes. Add chicken broth, nutmeg or allspice and pepper. Cook 10-15 minutes. Remove from heat and put in food processor fitted with steel blade or in blender. Puree till smooth. Put back on low heat and bring to boil. Remove from heat. Serve with yogurt and chives.

Pumpkin Soup
(Microwave)

8 lb. pumpkin, cut in half,
seeds and pulp removed
1/3 cup finely chopped
onion
1/4 cup butter
3 cups hot water
2 Tbsp. instant chicken
bouillon granules

1/4 tsp. nutmeg
1/8 tsp. white pepper
1/8 tsp. ginger
1/8 tsp. allspice
1 stick cinnamon
1/2 cup half & half

Place 1/2 of pumpkin in 8 x 8 inch baking dish. Cover with plastic wrap. Microwave at high for 10-15 minutes or till tender, rotating dish every 5 minutes. Repeat with remaining half. Spoon pumpkin from shell. Mash or process in food processor till smooth. Set aside. Place onion and butter in 5 quart casserole; cover. Microwave at high 3 to 5 1/2 minutes or till tender, stirring once. Mix in mashed pumpkin and remaining ingredients. Reduce power to 50% (medium). Microwave uncovered 8 to 10 minutes or until flavors blend, stirring 2 or 3 times. Spoon into 2 freezer containers. Label and freeze no longer than 2 months. To serve, remove from one container and place in 1 1/2 quart casserole. Microwave at 50% (medium) 17 to 21 minutes or till heated, breaking apart and stirring 2 or 3 times. Makes 2 soups, 4 to 6 servings each.

Pumpkin Bisque

1 (16 oz.) can pumpkin
1/3 cup sour cream dip
with chives

1 cup light cream
1/2 tsp. salt
2 cups chicken broth

In mixing bowl, combine pumpkin, sour cream dip, chicken broth, cream and salt; beat smooth with rotary beater. Cover and chill. Garnish with dollops of additional sour cream dip with chives, if desired. Makes 6 to 8 servings.

Creamy Pumpkin Soup
(Microwave)

1 cup hot water
3/4 cup canned pumpkin
3 Tbsp. thinly sliced
   green onions
2 tsp. frozen orange
   juice concentrate

1 1/2 tsp. low-sodium in-
   stant chicken bouillon
   granules
1/4 tsp. cinnamon
1/8 tsp. ginger
1/2 cup skim milk

In 1 quart casserole, combine all ingredients, except milk. Mix well. Cover. Microwave at high for 3 1/2 to 5 1/2 minutes or till bubbly and onions are just tender-crisp, stirring once. Stir in milk. Microwave at high for 30 seconds to 1 minute longer or till hot. Stir before serving.

Pumpkin Mushroom Soup

1/2 lb. mushrooms,
   sliced
1/2 cup chopped onion
2 Tbsp. butter or oil
2 Tbsp. flour
1 Tbsp. curry powder

3 cups chicken broth
salt and pepper
1 Tbsp. honey
dash nutmeg
1 (1 lb.) can pumpkin
1 cup evaporated milk

Sauté mushrooms and onion in oil. Add curry and flour, stir. Add broth gradually. Add everything but milk, cook, stirring 10-15 minutes. Add milk, heat through without boiling. Top with sour cream or yogurt, if desired. Serves 6.

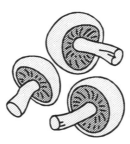

Meat Loaf in a Pumpkin

1 lb. hamburger or sausage	1 large onion, diced
6-8 slices bread, crumbled	1 small pumpkin
1 egg	1/2 tsp. salt

(Dry bread slices may be used–soak in a little water till soft, squeeze dry.)

Mix meat, bread, egg and onion well. Sprinkle a little salt on inside of cleaned pumpkin. Fill with meat loaf mixture. Bake at 375° for 1 1-2 to 2 hours. (Place pumpkin on a pan with a little water in it or place a pan of water on the shelf below.)

Beef Stew in a "Pumpkin Pot"

1/2 - 1 lb. beef cubes	1 small pumpkin
1 tsp. pepper	1 cup green beans
2-3 potatoes, diced	1 cup lima beans
1/2 lb. carrots, sliced	1 cup corn
3 Tbsp. cornstarch	1 stalk celery
1/2 tsp. salt	1 onion

Brown meat well in hot pan. Do not use grease, just turn the heat down a little when meat is added to pan. Turn when brown. When well-browned, pepper the meat, add 5-6 cups hot water. Cover and simmer 2-3 hours. Parboil potatoes, 10-15 minutes. Steam sliced carrots, 15 minutes. Mix the cornstarch with about 1/2 cup cold water, and stir into the beef broth. Sprinkle salt in the cleaned-out pumpkin. Add meat and vegetables. Put lid on pumpkin and bake at 375° for 1 1/2 - 2 hours (depending on size of pumpkin). When pumpkin is done, stew is ready to serve. Add cornstarch for thickening, if desired. You will scoop out some pumpkin with the stew when serving.

Note: vegetables may be varied–a few tomatoes, chopped cabbage, parsnips. Stew may be made a day ahead. Refrigerate. Put into pumpkin when ready to bake.

Mexican Stuffed Pumpkin

1 (3 to 5 lb.) pumpkin
2 cans enchilada sauce
1 cup water
2 slices bacon, chopped
1/2 cup chopped bell
  pepper
1 onion, chopped
2 cups chopped
  mushrooms
2 cloves garlic, mashed

salt and pepper
1 cup cooked sweet corn
1/2 cup sliced black ol-
  ives
3 cups cooked rice
1 can chili salsa or
  Mexican sauce
1 cup grated dry Parme-
  san or Romano cheese
2 eggs, beaten

Cut pumpkin and scoop center out, leaving a shell 1/2 inch thick. Pour enchilada sauce combined with water in large shallow pan and steam shell, covered with foil at 325° for 30 minutes. Sauté the bacon for 4 to 5 minutes. Add bell pepper, onion, mushrooms and garlic and cook till onion is clear. Remove. Add corn, olives, rice, chili salsa or Mexican sauce, beaten eggs and salt and pepper, and mix all together. Chop and combine pumpkin with stuffing. Scoop mixture into pumpkin shells; top with dry, grated cheese. Cover again with foil and bake until pumpkin shell is tender, to taste, approximately 30-45 minutes. Serves 8.

> *Pumpkins are a healthy addition
> to the diet as they are rich in
> phosphorous, calcium, iron
> and vitamins A and C.*

Pumpkin-Stuffed Pumpkin Shell

1 (4 to 6 lb.) pumpkin
1/2 lb. sweet or hot
   sausage (or mixture
   of both)
2 Tbsp. vegetable oil
2 medium onions,
   chopped
2 cloves garlic, minced

1 lb. coarsely chopped
   mushrooms
4 cups cooked rice
1 cup grated Parmesan
   cheese
1/2 cup finely chopped
   fresh parsley
1/2 tsp. thyme
2 eggs, slightly beaten

Preheat oven to 450°. Cut slice off top of pumpkin. Scoop out seeds and membrane. Pre-bake pumpkin in a pan filled with about 1 inch of water for about 30 minutes. Remove from oven and lower temperature to 375°. Remove casings from sausage. Chop and cook in 2 tablespoons oil till brown. Add onions and garlic; sauté until wilted. Add mushrooms and sauté until most of liquid has evaporated. Add rice, 1/2 cup of the cheese, parsley and thyme to ingredients in skillet. Mix well. Add eggs and mix again. Pack into pumpkin shell and sprinkle remaining cheese over top. Return pumpkin to oven and bake for 40 minutes.

Pumpkin-Ham Casserole

2 Tbsp. unsalted butter
1 medium onion, finely
  chopped
1 cup chopped ham
3 cups cubed, pared
  pumpkin
1 tsp. fresh lemon juice
2 tsp. minced fresh parsley
3/4 tsp. salt
1/2 tsp. ginger
1/8 tsp. freshly ground
  pepper
pinch ground cumin seed
1/3 cup sliced scallion
  tops

Melt butter in large pan over medium high heat. When foam subsides, add onion. Cook till softened, about 5 minutes. Add ham. Toss with spoon to combine. Add pumpkin, lemon juice, parsley, salt, ginger, pepper and cumin seed to pan. Stir to mix well. Cover pan. Cook till pumpkin is tender, about 15 minutes. Stir scallion tops into pumpkin mixture. Transfer to covered serving dish. Serve hot.

Pumpkin Vegetable Scallop

4 cups raw pumpkin
1 small onion
1 green pepper
2 Tbsp. butter
salt, pepper, and paprika
2 oz. buttered bread
  crumbs

Peel, steam, mash pumpkin. Cut onion and green pepper fine and brown in butter. Add to pumpkin and season with salt, pepper and paprika. Turn mixture into greased baking dish and cover top with buttered crumbs. Bake in moderately hot (325°) oven 20 minutes or until golden brown.

Pumpkin Soufflé

1/2 cup cold butter
1 cup flour
1 1/3 cups milk
6 eggs, room temperature, separated
1/2 cup canned pumpkin
2 Tbsp. honey
1/2 tsp. mace
1/2 tsp. ginger
1/2 tsp. nutmeg
1/2 tsp. cloves
1 tsp. cinnamon
1 1/2 tsp. grated orange zest (orange part of rind only; 1 orange)
confectioners sugar, optional
Calvados Creme Anglaise

Preheat oven to 375°. Grease and lightly flour a 1 1/2 quart soufflé dish. Break up butter in large pieces in large bowl. Add flour. Cut in butter with pastry blender or 2 forks. Bring milk to boiling in pan. Remove from heat. Whisk dough into milk until it is smooth. Place milk mixture in large bowl. Add egg yolks, pumpkin, spices, orange zest and honey and mix till well blended. Beat egg whites in a large bowl till medium peaks form. Gently fold 1/3 of whites at a time into pumpkin mixture. Pour pumpkin mixture into prepared soufflé dish. Bake in 375° oven for 50 minutes or till top is puffed and center barely moves when shaken. Sprinkle with powdered sugar if you wish. Serve with Calvados Creme Anglaise.

Calvados Creme Anglaise:

3/4 cup powdered sugar
1 cup milk
1 tsp. Calvados® or apple flavored brandy
4 egg yolks
1/2 tsp. vanilla

Stir together powdered sugar and egg yolks in a medium size bowl until well combined. Combine milk with vanilla in medium pan. Bring mixture just to boiling. Stirring constantly, add milk mixture to egg yolk mixture. Return to pan. Cook medium heat, stirring constantly, 2-3 minutes. Do not boil. Strain. Stir in Calvados or brandy.

Pumpkin Chiffon Soufflé

1 pkg. (6 3/4 oz.)
Pepperidge Farm®
Bordeaux cookies
2 Tbsp. butter, melted
3/4 cup brown sugar
2 envelopes unflavored
gelatin
1/2 tsp. cinnamon
1/2 tsp. nutmeg
1/2 tsp. allspice
1/4 tsp. ginger
1/4 tsp. salt
1 cup milk
4 eggs, separated
1 can (29 oz.) pumpkin
1/3 cup sugar
1/2 pt. whipping cream

Reserve 10 cookies. Crush remaining cookies to make crumbs and mix with melted butter. Combine brown sugar, gelatin, spices and salt in pan. Add milk to egg yolks and beat; stir in pumpkin. Add to brown sugar mixture, cook over low heat, stirring until gelatin is completely dissolved and mixture thickens slightly. Chill, stirring occasionally until mixture mounds slightly when dropped from a spoon. Beat egg whites until soft peaks form, gradually add sugar, beating after each addition until stiff. Fold into cooled pumpkin. Beat whipping cream till stiff and pour into pumpkin mixture. Pour just enough pumpkin filling into 2 quart heat-resistant glass soufflé dish to cover bottom. Stand reserved 10 cookies around sides of dish, spacing evenly. Carefully add filling, keeping cookies pressed around sides of dish. Sprinkle reserved cookie crumbs over top. Chill 4 hours or overnight.

In general, the smaller the pumpkin, the better the flavor.

And, some say, the bigger the pumpkin, the better the jack-o'-lantern!

Basic Pumpkin Soufflé

1 cup cooked pumpkin
1/2 tsp. cinnamon
1/2 cup brown sugar

3 egg whites
1/8 tsp. salt

To pumpkin, add cinnamon and sugar. Mix well. Beat egg whites till stiff. Add salt. Fold into pumpkin mixture. Fill greased baking dish or individual molds 2/3 full and set in pan of hot water. Bake at 350° about 40 minutes for large mold and 25-30 minutes for individual molds. Serves 6.

Pumpkin Spaghetti

1 cup solid pack pumpkin
1 cup heavy cream
1 cup grated Parmesan
   cheese
1/2 tsp. nutmeg

1/4 cup softened butter
12 oz. thin spaghetti,
   cooked and drained
freshly ground black
   pepper

Mix pumpkin, cream, 1/2 cup cheese and nutmeg in small pan. Bring just to simmer over low heat, stirring once or twice. Remove from heat. Add butter to spaghetti in large bowl. Toss till butter is melted. Pour pumpkin mixture over pasta. Toss. Transfer to serving dish. Season to taste.

To encourage pumpkin seeds to sprout quickly, soak them in lukewarm water the day before planting.

Pumpkin Italiano

2 Tbsp. vegetable oil
1 large onion, thinly
 sliced
2 1/2 cups fresh cubed
 pumpkin
1 1/2 lbs. ground beef
1 cup tomato sauce

1 clove garlic, minced
1/2 tsp. cinnamon
1/4 tsp. powdered ginger
salt and pepper to taste
1 cup cottage cheese
1 egg, beaten

Heat oil in medium pan and sauté onion until transparent. Add pumpkin and cook over medium-high heat until just tender. Transfer onion and pumpkin to a shallow casserole. In same pan, brown the beef. Pour off excess fat and stir in tomato sauce, garlic, cinnamon and ginger. Simmer 10 minutes. Add salt and pepper to taste. Spread the meat sauce over the pumpkin and onion. Mix together the cottage cheese and egg. Spread it over all. Bake at 350° for 30 minutes.

Pumpkin Chiffon Tarts

pastry for double pie
3/4 cup packed brown
   sugar
1 envelope unflavored
   gelatin
1 tsp. cinnamon
1/2 tsp. salt
1/4 tsp. nutmeg

1/4 tsp. ginger
3/4 cup milk
3 eggs, separated
1 1/4 cups canned
   pumpkin
3 egg whites
1/4 cup sugar

Prepare pastry, divide in half. Roll half the pastry at a time to 1/8 inch thickness. Cut each half into 5 (4 1/2 inch) circles. Fit over inverted muffin pans, pinching pleats at intervals to fit around pans. Prick pastry. Bake at 450° for 7 to 10 minutes or till golden. Cool. In pan, combine brown sugar, gelatin, salt and nutmeg and ginger. Stir in milk and egg yolks. Cook and stir till slightly thickened. Remove from heat; stir in pumpkin, chill to the consistency of corn syrup, stirring occasionally. Immediately beat egg whites till soft peaks form. Gradually add sugar, beating till stiff peaks form. When gelatin mixture is consistency of unbeaten egg whites (partially set), fold in stiff-beaten egg whites. Chill till mixture mounds when spooned. Turn into baked tart shell. Chill several hours or overnight till set. Cover. Chill to store. Makes 10 tarts.

*Pumpkin seeds have been
found in ancient Asian ruins and
in prehistoric Indian cliff dwellings
in Colorado.*

Apple Pumpkin Dessert

2-4 tart apples
1/4 cup raisins
1/4 - 1/2 cup chopped
  nuts
2 Tbsp. flour
2 tsp. cinnamon

1 tsp. nutmeg
1/4 tsp. ginger
1/4 tsp. cloves
1/4 - 3/4 cup sugar
1 small pumpkin

Slice apples, add raisins and nuts. Mix flour and spices and toss to coat fruit and nuts. Sprinkle 2 tablespoons - 1/4 cup sugar on inside of cleaned-out pumpkin. Add fruit and nut mixture and another 1/4 to 1/2 cup sugar. Put lid on pumpkin and bake at 375° for about 1 1/2 hours till pumpkin is tender. Scoop out some pumpkin with each serving. Serve with ice cream or half & half.

Raisin-Pumpkin Pudding

4 eggs
2 cups low fat cottage
  cheese
1/4 cup sugar

1 can (29 oz.) pumpkin
3/4 cup raisins
1/4 cup chopped pecans
ground cinnamon

Place eggs in electric blender; process until beaten. Add next 3 ingredients and process till smooth. Fold in raisins and pecans. Pour mixture into ungreased 12 x 8 x 2 inch baking dish. Sprinkle with cinnamon. Place baking dish in a larger pan; add warm water to larger pan to measure 3/4 inches. Bake at 350° for 45 minutes or until knife inserted in center comes out clean. Yield: 12 servings (about 127 calories each).

Pumpkin Pudding
(Microwave)

1/2 cup pecans, divided
3/4 cup vanilla wafer
  crumbs
1 Tbsp. sugar
1 tsp. grated orange rind
2 Tbsp. margarine,
  melted
1 (3 oz.) pkg. cream
  cheese, softened

1/2 cup firmly packed
  brown sugar
1/3 cup orange juice
3 eggs
1 tsp. grated orange rind
1/2 tsp. ground cardamon
1 cup cooked mashed
  pumpkin

Spread pecans in a single layer in a pie plate. Microwave at high 2 minutes stirring after 1 minute. Chop pecans; set aside. Combine 1/4 cup chopped pecans and next 4 ingredients, mixing well. Divide mixture into 8 (6 ounce) greased custard cups or ramekins. Press crumb mixture evenly in bottom of custard cups. Microwave at high 2 minutes; set aside. Beat cream cheese at medium speed of electric mixer till light and fluffy; gradually add brown sugar, mixing well. Add eggs and orange juice, mixing well. Add 1 teaspoon orange rind, cardamon and pumpkin, mix until smooth. Pour into prepared custard cups. Arrange cups in circle in oven. Microwave, uncovered at medium-high (70%) 6 to 7 minutes or till pudding is set, rearranging cups halfway through cooking time. Garnish with remaining 1/4 cup chopped pecans and, if desired, whipped cream, vanilla wafers or orange rind. Serve warm or chilled. 8 servings.

Baked Pumpkin Pudding

6 Tbsp. margarine
3/4 cup packed brown
  sugar
1/4 cup sugar
2 eggs
1 1/2 cups flour
3/4 cup pumpkin

1/2 cup buttermilk
1/2 tsp. salt
1/2 tsp. soda
1/2 tsp. cinnamon
1/2 tsp. ginger
1/4 tsp. nutmeg
1/2 cup chopped nuts

Cream margarine and sugars together till light; beat in eggs. Stir together flour, salt, soda, cinnamon, ginger and nutmeg. Combine pumpkin and buttermilk; add to creamed mixture alternately with dry ingredients, mixing well after each addition. Fold in chopped nuts. Spoon mixture into greased and floured 6 1/2 cup ring mold; cover tightly with foil. Bake at 350° for 1 hour. Let stand 10 minutes. Unmold. Serve with whipped cream, if desired. Makes 12-16 servings.

Pumpkin-Nut Pudding

2 1/2 cups light brown
    sugar
3 Tbsp. butter
1/4 cup water
4 cups pumpkin
1 tsp. salt
2 tsp. cloves
3 1/2 tsp. cinnamon

2 tsp. ginger
1/2 tsp. nutmeg
1 Tbsp. grated lemon rind
6 eggs
3 cups evaporated milk
3/4 - 1 cup broken nut
    meats

Put 3/4 cup sugar and butter in saucepan and cook over medium heat, stirring constantly until mixture comes to boil. Let boil 1 minute, still stirring, and add the water and boil 4 minutes. Place a 3 1/2 quart glass baking dish in a pan of hot water and pour in the sugar mixture. Tilt the dish immediately in all directions to coat the bottom and sides with caramel. Butter any uncovered spots. Set dish aside. Mix thoroughly the pumpkin, 1 3/4 cup sugar, salt, spices and lemon rind. Beat eggs with rotary beater 2 minutes and add to the pudding. Add milk and nuts and stir till well blended. Pour the mixture into the caramelized baking dish. Put the baking dish in a pan of hot water and bake in moderately slow oven, 325°, for 2 hours until the center is firm. When cool, chill overnight in refrigerator. Unmold the pudding by setting the dish in warm water and loosening with a spatula. Invert pudding onto platter, decorate top with nut meat halves and serve with a border of vanilla sauce and/or whipped cream. 12-16 servings.

Vanilla Sauce:

2 cups milk
6 Tbsp. sugar
1/4 tsp. salt

2 tsp. vanilla
4 egg yolks

Heat milk and vanilla. Combine sugar with egg yolks and salt. Pour little hot milk into sugar-egg mixture, blend well and then stir into hot milk. Heat in double boiler, stirring constantly until mixture coats spoon. Serve warm or cold.

Pumpkin Chiffon Dessert

1 3/4 cups crushed graham cracker crumbs
1/4 cup sugar
1/2 cup margarine, melted
8 oz. softened cream cheese
2 eggs, beaten
3/4 cup sugar
2 (3 3/4 oz.) pkg. instant vanilla pudding
3/4 cup milk
2 cups pumpkin
1/2 tsp. cinnamon
frozen whipped topping

Combine cracker crumbs, 1/4 cup sugar and margarine. Press into 13 x 9 x 2 inch pan. Set aside. Combine cream cheese, eggs and 3/4 cup sugar. Beat until fluffy. Spread over crust. Bake at 350° for 20 minutes. Set aside to cool.

Combine pudding and milk. Beat 2 minutes. Add pumpkin and cinnamon. Mix well. Stir in 1 cup frozen whipped topping. Spread over cream cheese layer. Spread top with remaining 1 cup of topping. Sprinkle with chopped pecans if desired. Serves 15.

Pumpkin Custard

1 1/2 cups canned pumpkin
2/3 cup brown sugar
3 beaten eggs
1 1/2 cups scalded milk
1 Tbsp. cornstarch
1 tsp. cinnamon
1/2 tsp. ginger
1/4 tsp. each cloves and nutmeg

Pour into buttered baking dish. Bake 45 minutes at 350°. Serves 4 to 6.

Pumpkin Custard

1 cup canned pumpkin
1/2 tsp. salt
2/3 cup half & half (milk and cream)
1 egg
pinch each of: allspice, ginger, nutmeg and cloves
3 tsp. butter or margarine
1/4 tsp. cinnamon
4 Tbsp. sugar

Beat all ingredients together. If possible use individual ramekins, otherwise a large soufflé dish or mold will do. Set in a pan in 1 inch of water. Bake 1 hour at 350°. Cool before serving. Yield: 4 servings.

Pumpkin Mousse

Whip 1 cup heavy cream to soft-peak stage. Fold into pumpkin-chiffon filling and turn into 6-cup soufflé dish with a paper collar to set. Sprinkle with finely chopped crystallized ginger root. Serves 8.

In eighteenth century New England, pumpkin shells were used for cutting hair. They were turned upside down over the prospect's head, and the hair was trimmed around the base of the shell.

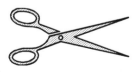

Pumpkin Flan

1 1/4 cups sugar, divided
1/4 tsp. salt
1 tsp. cinnamon
1 cup pumpkin
1 1/2 cups evaporated
 milk

5 eggs, beaten
1/3 cup water
1 1/2 tsp. vanilla
1/2 cup whipping cream
1 Tbsp. sugar
1/4 tsp. grated orange rind

Sprinkle 1/2 cup sugar evenly in a 9 inch cast iron skillet; place over medium heat. Caramelize sugar by stirring often until sugar melts and is light golden brown; pour immediately into a 9 inch cake pan, tipping pan quickly until the sugar is evenly spread. Combine 3/4 cup sugar, salt and cinnamon; stir well. Add pumpkin, milk, eggs, water and vanilla; stir until smooth. Pour over caramelized sugar, place cake pan in larger shallow pan. Pour about 1 inch of hot water in larger pan. Bake at 350° for 1 hour or until a knife inserted near center comes out clean. Remove pan from water; chill several hours or overnight. Loosen edges with a spatula. Place serving plate upside down on top of cake pan; quickly invert flan onto serving plate. Combine whipping cream, 1 table-spoon sugar and orange rind; beat till stiff peaks form. Serve with flan. Yield: 1 (9 inch) flan.

An alternative to a carved jack-o'-lantern, which spoils within a few days, is a whole pumpkin decorated with vegetables (such as a carrot nose) or with paint.

Frozen Pumpkin Dessert

1 cup graham cracker
   crumbs
1/2 cup sugar
4 Tbsp. butter
1/2 cup pumpkin
scant 1/2 cup brown
   sugar

1/2 tsp. salt
1 tsp. cinnamon
1/4 tsp. ginger
1/8 tsp. cloves
1/2 gal. vanilla ice
   cream, softened

Combine crumbs, sugar and butter in bowl and blend thoroughly. Sprinkle 3/4 of mixture in 9 inch spring form pan. Reserve 1/4 for topping. Combine remaining ingredients and mix well. Pour into pan and sprinkle with reserved topping. Freeze.

Pumpkin Alaska

1/2 lb. marshmallows
2 cups canned pumpkin
2/3 cup brown sugar
1 tsp. salt
1 1/2 tsp. ginger
1 1/2 tsp. cinnamon
2 Tbsp. boiling water

4 Tbsp. orange juice
4 egg yolks, beaten
1 1/2 cups heavy cream,
   whipped
1 baked pastry shell
6 egg whites
6 Tbsp. sugar

Melt marshmallows in top of double boiler. While melting, add pumpkin, sugar and salt. Mix ginger, cinnamon with boiling water, add to melting mixture, then add orange juice. When marshmallows are completely melted, remove from heat, add to egg yolks and beat till smooth. Pour into freezing tray and chill. When cold and slightly stiffened, fold into cream. Return to refrigerator and freeze. Mixture may be frozen in ice–salt pack. Just before serving, spread frozen mixture into pastry shell and cover with thick meringue made by beating egg whites until stiff, then beating in sugar gradually. Place pie under hot broiler to brown. Serve at once.

Pumpkin Mints

1/4 cup milk
4 tsp. butter
3 1/2 cups confectioners
   sugar

2-3 drops oil of peppermint
yellow food coloring
green food coloring
red food coloring

Heat milk and butter and stir till butter has melted. Add confectioners sugar. Mix thoroughly and add the oil of peppermint. Knead with hands until fondant is smooth. Take out about 1/6 and color it green. Knead to mix color evenly. Cover with damp cheesecloth to prevent drying. Add enough yellow and red coloring to the rest of the fondant to make it a nice orange pumpkin color. Cover with damp cheesecloth. Work with small amounts of the orange-colored fondant at a time and roll into small balls in the palms of your hands. Break a toothpick in 2 and make grooves in the fondant like those in a pumpkin, using the broken end of the toothpick. Roll a bit of the green fondant in thin cylinders and cut in short stem like pieces. Press on top of the pumpkins. Yield: 40 mints.

Pumpkin Dandies

1 cup pumpkin
1 cup sugar
1 1/4 cups flaked
  coconut, lightly packed
1/2 tsp. cinnamon

1/4 tsp. nutmeg
finely chopped walnuts
  or peanuts
red and green candied
  cherries, optional

In large, heavy saucepan, combine pumpkin, sugar, coconut and spices; mix well. Cook over medium-high heat, stirring constantly for about 15 to 20 minutes. Candy is done when it becomes very thick and leaves side of pan, forming a ball in center as you stir. Turn mixture onto a buttered baking sheet; cover loosely with foil or plastic wrap; let cool completely. Lightly butter hands and shape candy into balls; roll in chopped nuts. Top each with a candied cherry half, if desired. Cover and store in refrigerator. About 2 1/2 dozen.

Pumpkin Chocolate Candy

2 cups sugar
1/2 cup evaporated milk
2 Tbsp. canned pumpkin
1/4 tsp. cornstarch

1/2 tsp. pumpkin pie
  spice
1 cup chocolate chips
1/2 tsp. vanilla

In medium pan, combine sugar, milk, pumpkin, cornstarch, pumpkin pie spice and chocolate chips. Cook over medium heat, stirring constantly, until sugar is melted and mixture comes to a boil. Cook until a small amount dropped into cold water forms a soft ball (238°). Remove from heat; add vanilla. Beat until creamy. Pour into greased 8 x 8 x 2 inch pan. Cool until firm. Cut into squares.

Pumpkin Ice Cream

Scald in double boiler:

2 cups milk

Combine in bowl:

4 egg yolks or 2 eggs, beaten	**1/2 tsp. vanilla**
1 cup sugar	**2 tsp. cinnamon**
1/8 tsp. salt	**1 tsp. nutmeg**
2 cups canned pumpkin	**1/2 tsp. allspice**
	1/4 tsp. ginger

Add to hot milk and cook 4 minutes longer. Cool. Add:

1 cup cream
1 cup nuts, optional

Pour into freezer. Crank until stiff.

Pumpkin-Orange Butter

1 medium orange	**2 cups sugar**
1 3/4 cups (16 oz.) pumpkin	**1/4 cup lemon juice**

Carefully remove thin layer of peel from orange, making sure not to remove white portion. Reserve. Remove and discard remaining rind and seeds. Place reserved rind and orange pulp into blender jar; puree. (Should have about 1/2 to 3/4 cup.) Place in large saucepan with remaining ingredients. Heat to boiling over medium heat, stirring constantly, until thick, about 30 minutes. Pour into sterilized jars and process in boiling water bath or store covered in refrigerator. For spicy pumpkin butter, add 1 teaspoon nutmeg to butter after removing from heat.

Pumpkin Butter

After the pumpkin is stewed down as low as possible, to 1 gallon of pumpkin, use a quart of molasses and 1 pound of sugar. Cook until real thick and stir constantly to keep from burning. When done, add a teaspoon each of allspice, cinnamon and cloves. Put away in a cool place.

Pumpkin Butter

6 lbs. pumpkin
2 Tbsp. cinnamon
2 Tbsp. ginger
1 tsp. allspice

5 lbs. light brown sugar
5 lemons–juice and
    grated rind
2 cups water

Clean out and peel the pumpkin; put through fine blade of a food chopper. Add spices, sugar, lemon juice and rind. Let stand overnight. In morning, add the water, bring to a boil; cook gently until soft and clear. Continue to cook to desired consistency. Pour into hot jars and seal.

Pumpkin Preserve

Quarter a pumpkin; discard seeds and inner fibers. Slice, trim off outer skin and cut into 1/2 to 1 inch square pieces. To 5 pounds pumpkin, add 8 cups sugar; let stand overnight. In morning, add 3 thinly sliced lemons and 1/2 teaspoon salt. Bring to a boil; cook until pumpkin is clear and tender and the syrup thick. Pack in hot jars and seal.

Curried Mexican Pumpkin Seeds (Pepitas)

1/4 cup curry powder
1 1/4 cups water
1 clove garlic, crushed
1 1/2 tsp. salt
juice 1/2 lemon

2 cups salted pepitas
(Mexican pumpkin
seeds)
butter

Mix together in saucepan the curry, 1/4 cup warm water, garlic, 1 teaspoon salt and lemon juice. When well blended, add 1 cup water; then heat, stirring constantly, until mixture simmers. Add the pepitas and simmer for 5 minutes. Drain (save curry mixture for currying more pepitas), spread pepitas out on a baking sheet, dot with butter, sprinkle with 1/2 teaspoon salt and toast in very low oven, 275°, for about 1 hour, until they are crisp. Yield: 2 cups. (To curry more pepitas, mix 2 teaspoons curry into the remaining mixture, add water to make 1 1/2 cups of the mixture and repeat as before.)

Toasted Pumpkin Seeds

Wash 1 cup seeds and dry. Melt 1 tablespoon butter in a jelly roll pan; add seeds and coat by shaking pan. Place in 425° oven and toast 20 minutes until light and brown, stirring occasionally. Salt; cool and store in covered jar.

Pumpkin Seed Chews

Cook 1 cup shelled pumpkin seeds in 2 quarts water for 15 minutes with 1/2 cup salt substitute. Drain, but do not rinse. Dry slowly in warm oven.

Pumpkin Seeds

1 cup pumpkin seeds
1 tsp. Worcestershire
  sauce

1 Tbsp. melted margarine
salt or seasoning,
  as desired

Boil pumpkin seeds in water about 10 minutes. Drain well, spread on cookie sheet. Combine margarine, Worcestershire sauce and seasoning. Pour over pumpkin seeds. Bake at 350° for 30 minutes until nearly dry. May double or triple the recipe.

Pumpkin Pancakes

1 cup self-rising flour
1 Tbsp. sugar

1/2 tsp. cinnamon
1/4 tsp. nutmeg

Mix together, then combine and add **3/4 cup milk, 3/4 cup pumpkin** and **2 eggs.** Stir together and cook on a hot, greased griddle. It makes nice silver dollar size pancakes.

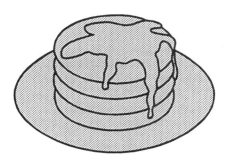

Pumpkin Event Sampler

Calabasas Pumpkin Festival (October)
Calabasas, CA • (818) 222-5680

Circleville Pumpkin Show (Always the 3rd week of Oct., Wed-Sat.)
Circleville, OH • (740) 474-7000

Crown Center Pumpkin Patch (October)
Kansas City, MO • (816) 274-8444

Great Halloween & Pumpkin Festival on West Portal
San Francisco, CA • (415) 249-4625

Half Moon Bay Art & Pumpkin Festival (October)
Half Moon Bay, CA • (650) 726-9652

Houston Pumpkin Festival
Houston, PA • (724) 745-1812

Morton Pumpkin Festival (September)
Morton Chamber of Commerce • Morton, IL • (309) 263-2491

National Pumpkin Festival (October)
Spring Hope, NC • (252) 459-4050

Ohio Pumpkin Festival (September)
Barnesville Area Chamber of Commerce • Barnesville, OH • (740) 425-4300

Pumpkinfest (1st weekend in October)
Anamosa Chamber of Commerce • Anamosa, IA • (319) 462-4879

Pumpkin Fest (October)
Confluence, PA • (814) 445-6431

Pumpkin Fest (October)
Kansas City, KS • (816) 792-2655

Pumpkin Fest (October)
Custer, WA • (306) 366-4372

Pumpkin Festival (October)
Lower Township, MN • (609) 463-6415

Pumpkin Festival (October)
Keene, NH • (603) 352-1303

Tuscola County Pumpkin Festival (October)
Caro Chamber of Commerce • Caro, MI • (517) 673-2511

World Pumpkin Confederation Weigh-Off (September)
Clarence, NY 14031 • (800) 449-5681

The Zeeland Pumpkin Festival (September-October)
Zeeland Chamber of Commerce, Zeeland, MI • (616) 772-2494

The 2002 Great Pumpkin Commonwealth (GPC) Weighoff Results
(Source: www.backyardgardener.com):

1. C. Houghton, NH — 1,337.6 lbs.
3. Greg Stucker, Elk Grove, CA — 1105 lbs.
2. Jerald Johnson, Clearbrook, MN — 1083 lbs.

If you would like your festival, activity or pumpkin patch included on these pages, please send the information to: Publicity Department **Golden West Publishers** • 4113 N. Longview, Phoenix, AZ 85014 (1-800-658-5830).

More Places to Enjoy Fall Activities

Adams Apple Orchard   www.upickvermont.com
1168 Old Stage Road • Williston, VT 05495   (860) 741-6324

Apple Basket Farms   www.applebasketfarms.com
RR1 Box 5 • Barry, IL 62312 .... (217) 335-2670

Apple Castle
Rt. 18 New Castle Sharon Rd. • New Wilmington, PA 16142 .... (724) 652-3221

Apple Crest Farm   www.applecrestfarm.com
133 Exeter Rd • Hampton Falls, NH 03844 .... (603) 926-3721

Applejack's Orchard
751 Brand Hollow Rd. • Peru, NY 12972 .... (518) 643-2268

Ashland Berry Farm's Memory Makers Weekend   www.richmondcity.com
12607 Old Ridge Rd • Beaverdam, VA 23015 .... (804) 227-3601

Belvedere Plantation   www.belvedereplantation.com
1601 Belvedere Dr. • Fredericksburg, VA 22408 .... (540) 373-4478

Bengtson Pumpkin Farm   www.pumpkinfarm.com
13341 W. 151st St. • Lockport, IL 60441 .... (708) 301-3276

Brookdale Farm
2060 Vaughan Rd. • Virginia Beach, VA 23457 .... (757) 721-0558

Burgers Farm & Garden Pumpkin Festival
7849 Main St.(State Rt. 32) • Cincinnati, OH 45244 .... (513) 561-8634

Carolyn's Country Cousins   www.carolynscountrycousins.com
17607 NE 52nd St. • Liberty, MO 64068 .... (816) 781-9196

Carroll's Pumpkin Farm   www.grinnelliowa.com/pumpkins
244 400th Ave.• Grinnell, IA 50112 .... (515) 236-7043

County Line Orchard   www.countylineorchard.com
200 County Line Rd. • Hobart, IN 46342.. (219) 947-4477

Curran's Orchard   www.curransorchard.com
6385 Kilburn (Rt. 70) • Rockford, IL 61101 .... (815) 963-7848

Deer View Orchard
64 Old Center Road N. • Deerfield, NH 03037 .... (603) 463-7549

Duncan's Sunfresh Farm's Pumpkin Patch   www.duncanfamilyfarms.com
17203 W. Indian School Rd • Goodyear, AZ 85240 .... (623) 853-0111

Eckert's Country Store & Farms   www.eckerts.com
Belleville, Millstadt and Grafton, IL .... (618) 233-0513

Eplegaarden   www.eplegaarden.com
2227 Fitchburg Rd. • Fitchburg, WI 53575 .... (608) 845-5966

Fall Family Fun on the Farm   www.engerfarm.com
RR 2 Box 68A • Hatton, ND 58240 .... (701) 543-3955

Faulkner Farm   www.faulknerfarm.com
14292 W. Telegraph Rd. • Santa Paula, CA 93060 .... (805) 525-2226

Finley's Orchard
2758 S. Madison Rd • Beloit, WI 53511 .... (608) 364-4175

Grandpa John's Farm & Pumpkin Patch
N.W. 4801 Hwy. 34 • Lincoln, NE 68524 .... (402) 470-2450

Gro-Moore Farms   www.gromoore.com
2811 E. Henrietta Rd. • Henrietta, NY 14467 .... (716) 359-3310

Hamilton Orchards
22 West St. • New Salem, MA 01355 .... (978) 544-6867

Happy Times Farm's Fall Family Day on the Farm
4965 Reynolds Rd. • Collierville, TN 38017 .... (901) 853-9642

Holmberg Orchard's Jack'O Lantern Jamboree   www.holmbergorchard.com
12697 325th St. • Vesta, MN 56292 .... (507) 762-3131

Jaswell's Farm
50 Swan Rd. • Smithfield, RI 02917 401-231-9043

Joe Huber Family Farm   www.joehubers.com
2421 Scottsville Rd. • Starlight, IN 47106 .... (812) 923-5255

More places to Enjoy Fall Activities *(continued)*

Just A Plain Farm www.justaplainfarm.com
5055 Gill Rd. • Carp Lake, MI 49718 .... (231) 537-2302

Landview Farms www.landview.net
2684 126th Ave. • Allegan, MI 49010 .... (616) 793-7593

Maze Quest at Maple Lawn Farms www.maplelawnfarms.com
2885 New Park Rd. • New Park, PA 17352 .... (800) 832-3697 ext. 102

Moser Farm & Market
69678 State Rd. 13 • Millersburg, IN 46543 .... (219) 642-5111

Mother Nature's Pumpkin Patch www.mothernaturesfarm.com
1663 E. Baseline Rd., Gilbert, AZ 85233 .... (480) 892-5874

Mystic Mountain Nursery
29908 Oso Loop Road • Arlington, WA 98223 .... (360) 435-5888

Nichols-Boyd Pumpkin Patch www.nichols-enterprises.com
3970 Hwy. 43 North • Brandon, MS 39047 .... (601) 829-9945

Petersen Farm's Pick Your Own Pumpkins
451 Putnam Pike • Chepachet, RI 02814 .... (401) 949-0824

Pick A Pumpkin Pumpkin Patch
2716 Creek Road • Esperance, NY 12066 .... (518) 868-4893

Pinehaven Farm www.pinehavenfarm.com
28040 Kettle River Blvd. • Wyoming, MN 55092 .... (651) 462-1704

Pinery Pumpkin Patch
10665 Brookview Lane • San Diego, CA 92131 .... (858) 566-7466

Pumpkin & Gourd Farm's Annual Pumpkin Events
101 Creston Road • Paso Robles, CA 93446 .... (805) 238-0624

Pumpkin City
Laguna Hills Mall — Sears Parking Lot • Laguna Hills, CA .... (949) 768-1103
Puente Hills Mall — Sears Parking Lot • Puente Hills, CA .... (949) 768-1103

Pumpkin Patch, The
10043 Highway 89 • Jay, FL 32565 .... (850) 675-1308

Pumpkins Etc.
E. of Platte City via Hwy. HH & Farmer's Ln.•Platte City, MO 64079 . (816) 858-5758 (eve.)

Reed Valley Orchard www.reedvalleyorchard.com
239 Lail Lane • Paris, KY 40361 .... (859) 987-6480

Roba's Pumpkin Patch www.robastreefarm.com
RR 1, Box 247 Decker Rd. • Dalton, PA 18414 .... (570) 563-2904

Shaw's Fruit & Produce Email: donnah@televar.com
3533 A. Hwy. 155 • Coulee Dam, WA 99116 .... (509) 633-0133

Schnepf Farm's Annual Pumpkin & Chili Party www.schnepffarms.com
22601 E. Cloud Road • Queen Creek, AZ 85242 .... (480) 987-3333

Sunny Crest Farm
59 High Range Rd. • Londonderry, NH 03053 .... (603) 432-7753

Swan's Pumpkin Farm's Fall Festival www.thepumpkinfarm.com
5930 Highway H • Franksville, WI 53126 .... (262) 835-4885

Tanners Orchard www.tannersorchard.com
740 State Route 40 • Speer, IL 61479 .... (309) 493-5442

Tweite's Pumpkin Patch & Mercantile www.tweite.com
1821 Frontier Rd. SW • Byron, MN 55920 .... (507) 634-4848

Vala's Pumpkin Patch www.valaspumpkinpatch.com
12102 S. 180th St. • Gretna, NE 68028 .... (402) 332-4200

Walters' Pumpkin Patch Email: BCWALTERS@prodigy.net
10001 NW 77 Hwy. • Burns, KS 66840 .... (316) 320-4150

Wauconda Orchards Inc. www.waucondaorchards.com
1201 Gossell Rd. • Wauconda, IL 60084 .... (800) 362-7753

Whittier Fruit Farm's Pumpkin Harvest www.whittierfruitfarm.com
219 Whittier Rd. • Rochester, NY 14624 .... (716) 594-9054

Wright's Mill Tree Farm Pumpkin Hunt www.wrightsmillfarm.com
63 Creasey Rd. • Canterbury, CT 06331 .... (860) 774-1455

Young's Farm's Pumpkin Festival www.prescottazindex.com
Junction Hwy 69 & Hwy 169 • Dewey, AZ 86327 .... (520) 632-7272

Favorite Pumpkin Recipes Index